Hallowed Ground

✴ ✴ ✴

Preserving America's Heritage

ABOVE View of Rappahannock County from Red Oak Mountain.

PAGES 2-3 Legend has it that Thoroughfare Gap, and adjacent features such as Leathercoat Mountain and Biscuit Mountain, were named by George Washington, who surveyed the area for Lord Fairfax. The gap was strategically crucial to Civil War armies; Stonewall Jackson's corps marched through it in August 1862 to strike the Union army from the rear and set the stage for Confederate victory at the Battle of Second Manassas.

PAGES 4-5 Denied communion for engaging in "touch dancing," some parishioners from Grace Episcopal Church in The Plains revolted against their rector in 1887 and founded the Church of Our Savior in nearby Little Georgetown. The dancing dispute resolved, Grace Church was reunited some years later. Today, its congregation maintains the small church at Little Georgetown and conducts a memorial service there each year.

PAGES 6-7 Surrounded by some of Virginia's most productive livestock farms, the Fauquier Livestock Exchange at Marshall hosts weekly auctions; area farmers sell 50,000 head of cattle every year. Similar sale barns operate at Orange, Culpeper, Front Royal, Winchester, and Nokesville, selling horses as well as cattle.

PAGES 8-9 Members of the Oakrum Baptist Church, near the village of Thoroughfare, lift their voices in hymns sung by the church congregation since 1865. Descendants of the church's founders still occupy pews that have been used by their families across the decades. Thoroughfare is one of several Piedmont communities founded by freedmen and former slaves.

PAGES 10-11 Hedgerows across a cattle farm in western Prince William County provide habitat for wildlife, help control erosion, and embellish the landscape. Once a feature of every farm, hedgerows have tended to disappear as smaller family farms have been consolidated into huge holdings where increasingly large and efficient equipment is used to plow, plant, and harvest.

PAGES 12-13 During most of the Civil War, Piedmont villages such as Hillsboro, in northern Loudoun County, were frequented by both Union and Confederate troops. Some of the homes where officers found food and shelter during the war years still stand, and in Hillsboro they help create an atmosphere of tranquility.

Hallowed Ground

★ ★ ★

Preserving America's Heritage

Rudy Abramson

Photographs by Kenneth Garrett and Jack Kotz

LICKLE PUBLISHING INC

Painted ceiling detail, New Ebenezer Church, Loudoun County

Published in 1997 by Lickle Publishing Inc
Copyright © 1996 Lickle Publishing Inc

Photographs copyright © 1996 by Kenneth Garrett
and Jack Kotz, as attributed on page 192.
Text copyright © 1996 Rudy Abramson

Art Director: Leonard Phillips
Editor: Deborah Sussman
Assistant Editor: Nancy Kober

Printed in Hong Kong

All enquiries should be directed to:
Lickle Publishing Inc
590 Madison Avenue, 26th floor
New York, NY 10022
[212] 371-5444

Library of Congress Cataloging-in-Publication Data

Abramson, Rudy
    Hallowed Ground: Preserving America's heritage/
Rudy Abramson: photographs by Kenneth Garrett and
Jack Kotz.
        p.   cm.
    Includes bibliographical references and index.
    ISBN 0-9650308-6-5 [hardcover]
    1. Piedmont [U.S. : Region]—Pictorial works. 2.
Piedmont [U.S. : Region]—History, Local. 3.
Virginia—Pictorial works. 4. Virginia—History, Local.
I. Garrett, Kenneth. II. Kotz, Jack. III. Title.
F227A27   1996
975—dc20
                                    96-24513

Page 31: Excerpt from the June 20, 1994 *New Republic*
article "A Mickey Mouse Idea" by C. Vann Woodward.
Page 81: Excerpt from *The Oxford History of the American
People*, copyright © 1965 by Samuel Eliot Morison. Page
110: Excerpt from *My Heart Is So Rebellious: The Caldwell
Letters, 1861–1865*, copyright © Bell Gale Chevigny,
courtesy of the Fauquier National Bank. Pages 123 and
127: Excerpts from the diary of Edward Carter Turner,
courtesy of the Virginia Historical Society, Richmond,
Virginia.

Table of Contents

Foreword

The gently rolling hills and valleys of Virginia's northern Piedmont cover an area of about three thousand square miles. Bounded roughly by

Kenmore—splendidly modern in 1776.

Charlottesville, Fredericksburg, Manassas, Leesburg, and Upperville, this part of the country is home to more history than any other area several times its size in the United States. Here lived Thomas Jefferson, James Madison, James Monroe, John Marshall, and other architects of a new nation. Here were fought some of the bloodiest battles in a terrible war that determined the fate of that nation: First and Second Manassas, Fredericksburg, Chancellorsville, Brandy Station, Bristoe Station, the Wilderness, and Spotsylvania, as well as lesser battles in which thousands gave their last full measure of devotion. Indeed, within the Piedmont lie no fewer than sixteen Civil War battlefields, thirteen historic towns, and seventeen historic districts.

This beautiful and historic locale became the focus of international attention in 1993, when the Walt Disney Company declared its intention to build an American-history theme park and surrounding real-estate development near Haymarket, Virginia. The announcement sparked enormous debate inside and outside Virginia about the impact of the proposed development on the Piedmont and its residents. Eventually, a coalition of historians, environmentalists, and concerned Americans from all walks of life persuaded Disney to withdraw its plans for a theme park at Haymarket. It was a responsible decision by a corporation which became convinced that it must not jeopardize the preservation of real history in order to present simulated history.

Unfortunately, the pressures for suburban development and urban sprawl in this region have not gone away with Disney's departure. They will undoubtedly get worse. One of the last large, unspoiled rural areas in the vast megalopolis stretching from Boston to Petersburg remains under threat.

The Civil War devastated the northern Virginia Piedmont. Armies fought, camped, and marched back and forth through the region for nearly four years. Woodlands disappeared, fields grew up in weeds and scrub, fences vanished, farms and homes were burned or abandoned. But the region recovered. Trees grew again, fields and pastures were cleared and planted, fences, homes, and farms were rebuilt. The northern Virginia Piedmont helped show the way for the rebuilding of a reunited America after the Civil War. If Thomas Jefferson were to ride over this area today, as he did many times between Charlottesville and Washington two hundred years ago, he would still recognize much of it.

Although the region recovered from the Civil War, it could never recover from the blacktop and concrete revolution that threatens it today. To pave over the northern Piedmont would pave over much of America's past—permanently. But that does not have to happen. If they are wisely planned, growth and preservation can march hand in hand. This eloquently written and beautifully illustrated book chronicles the important past and outlines a sensible future for the region. Hallowed ground it is; hallowed ground it can and must remain as it moves forward into the twenty-first century.

James M. McPherson
Edwards Professor of American History
Princeton University

If they are wisely planned, growth and preservation can march hand in hand.

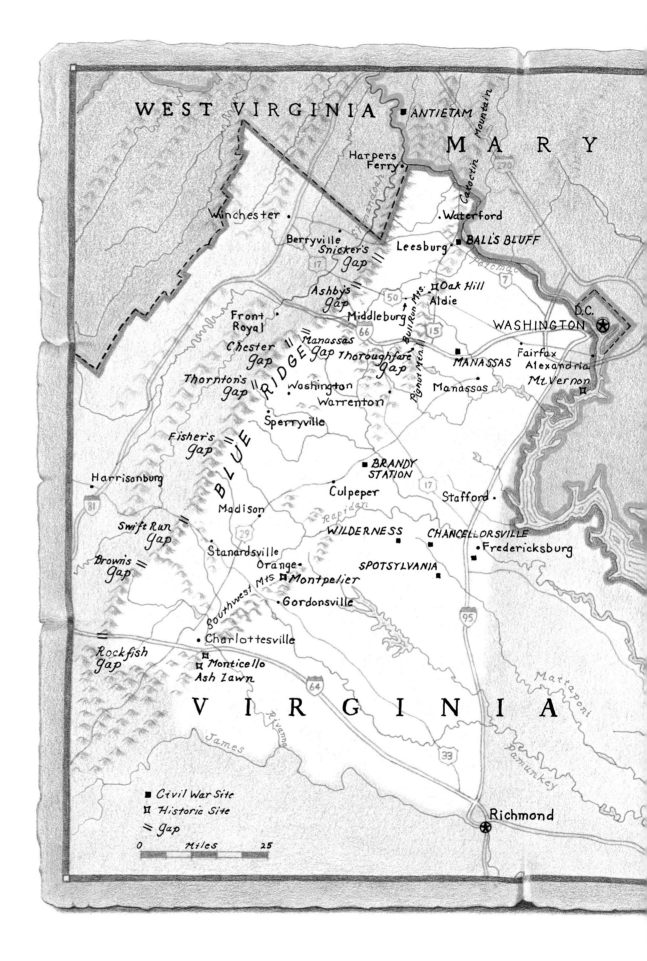

WEST VIRGINIA • ANTIETAM

MARY

Harpers Ferry •

Catoctin Mountain

• Waterford

Winchester • Leesburg • ■ BALL'S BLUFF

Berryville • Snicker's Gap

Ashby's Gap

⊞ Oak Hill
• Aldie

Front Royal

Middleburg

Bull Run Mts.

WASHINGTON ✪ D.C.

50

66

15

Chester Gap

Manassas Gap Thoroughfare Gap

■ MANASSAS

Fairfax
Alexandria

Mt. Vernon ⊞

Thornton's Gap

BLUE RIDGE

Washington

Pignut Mtn.

• Manassas

Warrenton

Sperryville •

Fisher's Gap

■ BRANDY STATION

Harrisonburg •

Culpeper •

17

Stafford •

81

Madison •

Rapidan

Swift Run Gap

29

WILDERNESS

CHANCELLORSVILLE

• Fredericksburg

Brown's Gap

Stanardsville •

Orange •
Southwest Mts.

⊞ Montpelier

SPOTSYLVANIA

• Gordonsville

95

Rockfish Gap

• Charlottesville

⊞ Monticello
Ash Lawn

64

Rivanna

VIRGINIA

33

James

Mattaponi

■ Civil War Site
⊞ Historic Site
= Gap

0   Miles   25

Pamunkey

Richmond ✪

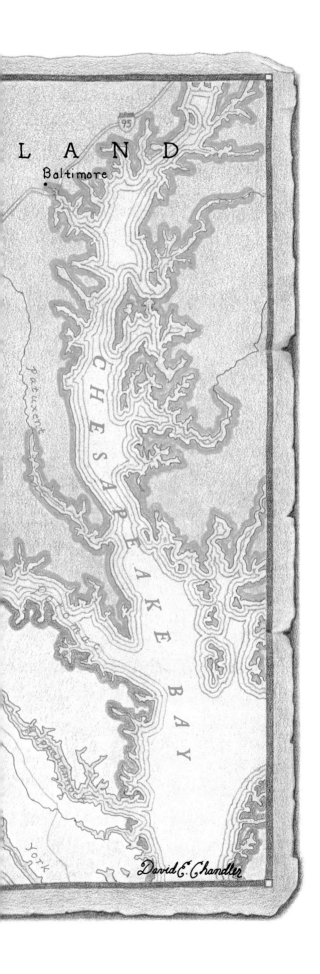

THE VIRGINIA PIEDMONT belongs to a hilly region lying between the flatland of America's eastern coastal zone and the Appalachian mountain system, which extends from New England into Georgia and Alabama. In northern Virginia, it is about 50 miles wide; in the southern part of the state it is about 125 miles across. This book concerns the hill country of northern Virginia, the picturesque and historically rich land between the falls of the Potomac and the Rappahannock Rivers and the Blue Ridge. Home to Washington, Jefferson, Madison, and Monroe, a killing ground of the Civil War, this small corner of the Old Dominion is one of the nation's natural and historic treasures.

On the 4,000-acre estate around his Oak Hill mansion in Loudoun County,
President James Monroe, using both slave labor and indentured servants,

raised livestock and planted a variety of crops. After completing his second
term in 1825, he retired here. Oak Hill remains privately owned.

Thomas Jefferson's Monticello, an American treasure.

A Masterpiece of Nature

✳ ✳ ✳

I N OCTOBER 1783, SEVERAL DAYS AFTER LEAVING MONTICELLO FOR Philadelphia and the reconvening of the Continental Congress, Thomas Jefferson and his daughter, Martha, arrived in the gorge where the Potomac and Shenandoah Rivers cut through the mountains and converge into one mighty stream. The squire of Monticello had crossed the Blue Ridge west of Charlottesville and proceeded north through the picturesque Shenandoah Valley and the thriving town of Winchester. Although he was an extensive traveler, this was Jefferson's first occasion to visit the river junction called Harpers Ferry.

A ferry service had been in operation there for more than fifty years, since the days when frontiersmen referred to the place as "the hole." When Jefferson arrived, the settlement still consisted of nothing more than a stone tavern, three dwellings, two mills, and a few outbuildings. After finding accommodations at the tavern, Jefferson climbed a steep path ascending a bluff behind it. On a lip of the mountain, he came upon a huge rock providing an unobscured view of the rivers below. Before him, he later wrote in *Notes on the State of Virginia,* was "one of the most stupendous scenes in nature," which he declared to be "worth a voyage across the Atlantic."

> You stand on a very high point of land. On your right comes up the Shenandoah, having ranged along the foot of the mountain a hundred miles to seek a vent. On your left approaches the Potomac, in quest of a passage also. In the moment of their junction, they rush together against the mountain, rend it asunder, and pass off to the sea. The first glance of this scene hurries our senses into the opinion that this earth has been created in time, that the mountains were formed first, that the rivers began to flow afterwards, that in this place, particularly, they have been dammed up by the Blue Ridge of mountains, and have formed an ocean which filled the whole valley; that continuing to rise they have at length broken over this spot, and have torn the mountains down from its summit to its base. The piles of rock on each hand, but particularly on the Shenandoah, the evident marks of their disrupture and avulsion from their beds by the most powerful agents of nature, corroborate the impression. But the distant finishing, which nature has given to the picture, is of a very different char-

acter. It is a true contrast to the foreground. It is as placid and delightful as that is wild and tremendous. For the mountain being cloven asunder, she presents to your eye, through the cleft, a small catch of smooth, blue horizon, at an infinite distance in the plain country, inviting you, as it were, from the riote and tumult roaring around, to pass through the breach and participate in the calm below.

The inviting "plain country" beyond the horizon and off toward Jefferson's Monticello estate was the Piedmont region of northern Virginia, 150 miles of "placid and delightful" hills and valleys.

Jefferson's famous description of the Shenandoah's dramatic meeting with the Potomac was considered a great exaggeration by many of his contemporaries. But Jefferson was a man with a passionate love for nature, and the entire northern Virginia region moved him to rhapsody. In all the world, he said, he knew of "no condition happier than that of a Virginia farmer" in the Piedmont.

ABOVE The view from Harpers Ferry. In the distance, bordered by the Potomac, lies the Piedmont of northern Virginia.

OPPOSITE Viewing the confluence of the Potomac and Shenandoah Rivers from this rock at Harpers Ferry, Thomas Jefferson was inspired to write a tribute to the natural beauty of Virginia.

At Monticello, he wrote his friend Maria Cosway, he could "ride above the storms" and "look down into the workhouse of nature, to see her clouds, hail, snow, rain, thunder, all fabricated at our feet! And the glorious Sun, when rising as if out of distant water, just gilding the tops of the mountains, and giving life to all nature!"

To other correspondents, he exalted over the area's "delicious spring," its "soft genial temperature," and its good soil. Indeed, he said his travels had convinced him "that these mountains are the Eden of the US for soil, climate, navigation, and health."

On the east, Virginia's northern Piedmont meets the Tidewater country along a zone roughly defined by modern Interstate 95 connecting Washington, D.C., and Richmond. Here, rocks hardened by the heat and pressure of mountain-building episodes give way to sedimentary deposits left by a prehistoric sea. In this transition zone, rivers originating in the Blue Ridge and cutting across the Piedmont highlands on their way to the Chesapeake Bay rush over their last rapids and settle into a deeper, more leisurely course to journey's end. At these rapids ended Captain John Smith's first expeditions to the interior of Virginia. In 1607 and 1608, his ships were halted by sharp rocks, and he was forced to run back down the James, the Rappahannock, and the Potomac.

From the hilly country between the coastal plain and the Blue Ridge mountains came an extraordinary number of America's founders. Upon this gentle landscape unfolded conflict and tragedy. Here occurred defining events of the nation's creation, testing, and renewal. Not surprisingly, this niche of the Old Dominion has come to be referred to as the very cradle of democracy.

ABOVE Montpelier, seat of the Madison family in Orange County, was greatly changed and modernized during private ownership in the twentieth century. First constructed in 1760, the house was inherited by the fourth President in 1801. It now belongs to the National Trust for Historic Preservation.

OPPOSITE James Monroe in his garden at Ash Lawn-Highlands. Jefferson's neighbor sold his Albemarle County plantation and moved north to Oak Hill in Loudoun County because the latter was closer to Washington.

The Piedmont was home to Jefferson, James Madison, James Monroe, and the great Chief Justice John Marshall. George Washington, whose Mount Vernon estate was just beyond the Piedmont in lower Fairfax County, surveyed much of the northern Virginia hill country and owned land in it. Washington's neighbor, George Mason, is generally recognized as the father of the U.S. Bill of Rights. These six men, whose words and deeds underpin more than two centuries of democratic government, were born in a radius of scarcely more than a hundred miles, and their lives were politically, socially, and personally intertwined.

Altogether, Washington, Jefferson, Madison, and Monroe occupied the presidency for thirty-two of the nation's first thirty-six years. Jefferson, Madison, and Monroe also served as secretary of state, and Jefferson was vice president for four years. By the end of the "Virginia dynasty," the United States had grown from a cluster of breakaway seaboard colonies into a continental power.

But the region that produced the intellectual ferment of the Revolution and a generation of leaders for the new nation would become a bloody testing ground for democracy.

With the Civil War, the Piedmont turned into a killing field, a bitterly contested, strategically priceless avenue between the capital of the United States and the capital of the Confederacy. Appalling bloodshed added names such as Manassas, Chancellorsville, Spotsylvania, Fredericksburg, and the Wilderness to the lexicon of warfare.

Every county, every community, and nearly every family in the Piedmont was swept into the conflict and indelibly scarred by it. When marching armies had come and gone, the Piedmont's war continued in incessant skirmishes among patrols, partisans, and night riders. Loudoun

ABOVE In Fredericksburg's city cemetery, half a mile from Marye's Heights, where Union soldiers are buried, lie more than 3,000 Confederates. Among them are six Confederate generals, and one Union general, Daniel Davis Wheeler, who won the Medal of Honor during the Battle of Chancellorsville and married a Fredericksburg woman after the war.

OPPOSITE One of many cannons on display at Manassas National Battlefield Park.

County especially was the scene of civil warfare in its most elemental form. It contained communities where loyalty to the Union ran deep, where many found slavery abhorrent, and where some even fought for the Union. In such places, neighbors became enemies, churches split, and families disintegrated.

The war claimed slaves and slave owners, old and young, rich and poor. In the contested land, there were no victors, only survivors. The recovery took decades. Some communities would not return to their prewar population for half a century. Reminders of the fighting are visible all across the region today. The countryside itself is a living museum.

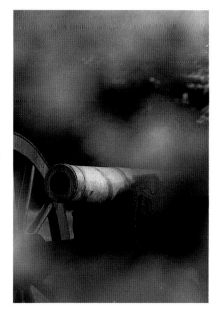

In the Fredericksburg vicinity alone, opposing armies suffered 100,000 casualties, more than those of the Indian wars, the Revolution, the War of 1812, and the War with Mexico combined. They are honored by fields of tombstones where many of them fell. And far from the major military cemeteries and churchyards where thousands are memorialized, lie the dead from isolated skirmishes, casualties from a decimated generation.

"This part of northern Virginia has soaked up more of the blood, sweat, and tears of American history than any other part of the country," C. Vann Woodward, the eminent Yale University historian, wrote in 1994. "It has bred more founding fathers, inspired more soaring hopes and ideals and witnessed more triumphs, failures, victories, and lost causes than any other place in the country."

Because of this rich history and magnificent natural wealth, the Piedmont survives as one of the treasures of rural America. Succeeding generations have passed along homesteads, farms, and communities much as they received them. But the region is increasingly threatened—this time by relentless, aimless, accelerating urban sprawl.

✳✳✳

AT THE TIME JEFFERSON STOOD MUSING above Harpers Ferry, scientists knew little about the origins of the mountains, the rivers, or the Piedmont. Today, the story is known to be exquisitely complex, and the natural history continues to challenge scholars just as it fascinated Jefferson.

After a century of research, scientists are still working to unravel the geological events that created the Appalachian range and surrounding foothills and valleys. For decades, they have known that North America's eastern mountains, including Virginia's Blue Ridge, are remarkably ancient, even by geological reckoning. It is now clear that the entire range was formed by recurring upheavals over the eons, and that these mountains were once far more imposing than they are today. In its youth, the Blue Ridge may have towered higher than the present day Rockies or the Himalayas. But by the time the first human migration reached the Piedmont some twenty thousand years ago, wind, rain, fire, ice, and relentless chemical and biological weathering had reduced snow-covered peaks to the familiar ridges now wrapped in hardwood forests and crowned by rhododendron and mountain laurel.

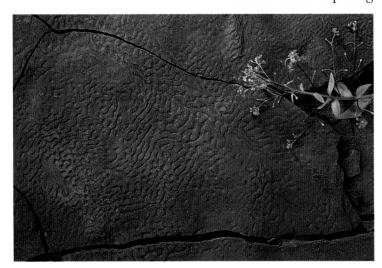

ABOVE A fingerprint from prehistory: a fossilized dinosaur skin found on the Oak Hill estate where James Monroe lived in retirement.

OPPOSITE On the west, the fabled Blue Ridge Mountains look down upon the Piedmont. National scenic treasures, they are among the oldest peaks in North America. The gentle ridge seen from The Plains may once have towered higher than the Rockies.

Evidence of the region's extreme age is indisputable. In the Loudoun Valley west of Leesburg between the Catoctin Mountains and the Blue Ridge, geologists have found rocks more than a billion years old, far older than the mountains themselves. These so-called "basement rocks" are the oldest ever uncovered in Virginia and among the most ancient ever found on the North American continent, fragments of the Appalachians' ancestors, thrust to the surface from the basement of time.

They were created during a period of mountain building that took place before there was any hint of life on earth. During the Grenville Orogeny, as the episode is known, barren continental masses—including rough approximations of what evolved into North America, Africa, and Europe—collided to form one gigantic supercontinent. At various places the crust buckled under the stupendous pressure. Rock from far below the surface was pushed upward, forming towering mountains.

After an interlude of 300 to 400 million years, the pieces of this supercontinent, under stresses within the earth, came apart. As they separated farther and farther, a proto-Atlantic Ocean, called the Iapetus Sea, was created between them. Beneath that shallow, prehistoric sea lay what is now the eastern United States, including the Virginia Piedmont.

In time, the land masses and the underlying tectonic plates floating on the earth's mantle again converged. Additional collisions closed the Iapetus, jostling the continents and stray plates against one another, and setting off new episodes of mountain building.

The Taconic Orogeny took place some 450 million years ago. The Acadian Orogeny occurred 75 million years after that. Finally, came the Alleghenian,

250 million years ago. The southern Appalachians, including the Blue Ridge, the Alleghenies, the Cumberlands, and the Great Smoky Mountains of Tennessee and North Carolina, are the product of this last collision.

When the supercontinent last separated, the tectonic waltz created the modern Atlantic Ocean. And as the seafloor spread, deep rift valleys were created in the region that is now the Piedmont. Over tens of millions of years, materials eroding from the mountains filled the valleys and created the modern highlands between the much diminished peaks and the coastal plain.

Some of these former rift valleys—the Barboursville and Culpeper basins—underlie the northern Piedmont. They extend from the neighborhood of Frederick, Maryland, to the Culpeper area, cutting across eastern Loudoun, western Fairfax, Prince William, Fauquier, and Culpeper Counties.

Outside the Culpeper County town of Stevensburg, a deep stone quarry has yielded striking evidence of prolific life in the basins 200 million years ago. There, workers encountered a six-acre area marked by no fewer than two thousand dinosaur tracks, most of them left by a three-toed carnivorous bird called dilophosaurus. The creatures walked the region between the young mountains and the retreating sea, and paleontologists have concluded that they fed at a shallow lake at the site of the modern quarry. Their tracks were preserved as the wetland periodically dried out and reflooded.

Today, the Atlantic continues to widen, and the Appalachians and the undulating Piedmont continue to erode. In another 50 million years, scientists estimate, the region's decorous ridges will be as flat as the coastal plain along the sea.

The finishing touches have been put on the modern Piedmont landscape by forces far less dramatic than the stresses that created the Blue Ridge. The Bull Run Mountains and the Pignut Mountains in Loudoun and Fauquier Counties and the Southwest Mountains near Charlottesville were created by erosion. Known to geologists as monadnocks, these ridges stand above the surrounding countryside because the terrain around them, composed of softer rock, has eroded away through the ages.

ABOVE The Southwest Mountains of Albemarle County. In Jefferson and Madison country, portions of a magnificent landscape remain unspoiled.

OPPOSITE The Piedmont and Tidewater meet where the soft sedimentary rock of the coastal zone hits rock hardened during episodes of mountain building over the eons. On streams such as the Rappahannock, the meeting is dramatized by river falls. Here swift streams from the uplands widen and begin a languid journey on to the Atlantic.

There are similar features along the length of the entire Piedmont. Extending from New York to Alabama in the shape of an elongated *S*, the distinctive region includes four state capitals in addition to Richmond. In the South, it fans out to a width of 150 miles or more; in northern Virginia, the average distance from the mountains across the plateau to the coastal plain is only about 50 miles.

In the areas where the Piedmont is broad and less hilly, the transition from the hard rock to the sedimentary deposits of the coastal plain causes little disruption. But in northern Virginia, the river falls marking the meeting of the Piedmont and the coastal zone are sometimes spectacular, and occasionally even dangerous.

The James River changes quickly from a free-flowing river into an estuary of the Chesapeake Bay as it passes Richmond. At Fredericksburg, the bridge crossing the Rappahannock on U.S. Highway 1 provides an impressive snapshot of the meeting of the Piedmont and the coastal plain. On the upstream side of the bridge, a swift, shallow river rushes over and around protruding rocks. Immediately on the downstream side of the bridge, it becomes the deeper, more peaceful stream that made Fredericksburg and Falmouth important port cities of colonial times.

The falls of the Potomac present a breathtaking and perilous barrier to

navigation. At Great Falls, 10 miles upstream from Washington, D.C., the river crashes down a drop of 77 feet in just three-quarters of a mile, cascading through one cataract 35 feet high. A little farther on, at Little Falls, it drops another 38 feet in 2 miles before finally reaching the languid estuary near Washington for the last 117 miles of its journey to the Chesapeake. Adventurers frequently underestimate the power and treachery of the rapids. Over the years, many people have died in the foaming current.

PAGES 36-37 Summer drought exposes the Great Falls of the Potomac, one of the most dramatic features along the fall zone where the Tidewater and Piedmont meet.

✳ ✳ ✳

AS LONG AS THE PIEDMONT HAS BEEN INHABITED, its culture has been powerfully influenced by its geology. The falls, river valleys, and gaps in the mountain ridges largely determined the way Native Americans lived in the region.

Long before the settlement of Jamestown, the fall line that blocked John Smith's passage separated the Native Americans of the Piedmont and the Tidewater. Below the river rapids lived the Algonquian-speaking Powhatans. Above the falls in the Piedmont were the Manahoacs, Monacans, Saponis, and other members of a far-flung family of Siouan-speaking tribes.

Although they concentrated in villages along the rivers, the Piedmont's Indian inhabitants farmed, hunted, and fished across the region, and their activities would influence the settlement patterns of Europeans who first came to the frontier. Where the Indians had burned forests to create grazing for buffalo, European settlers would plant tobacco, wheat, and corn. Former Indian settlements would become sites for mills. Hunting trails would become "rolling roads" for tobacco farmers, routes for flour wagons, and eventually turnpikes.

While the region was still a wilderness, a cultural revolution began. The people who had occupied and used the land for centuries had left it virtually unchanged. But its new citizens, the English, Germans, Scotch-Irish, and Quakers, would transform it within a few decades, and the changes they began would accelerate with each passing generation.

ABOVE The first English explorers to reach the Piedmont encountered natives who lived in villages near the river falls. Centuries before the arrival of white men, a native inhabitant created a message in stone, identifying a prime fishing spot on the upper Potomac.

RIGHT From the earliest settlement, travelers headed west to the Blue Ridge and farmers bound for ports on the Potomac passed through Thoroughfare Gap, a natural opening in the Bull Run Mountains of Prince William, Fauquier, and Loudoun Counties. The once narrow passage now accommodates both Virginia's Route 55 and Interstate 66.

Farmers from the Tidewater brought tobacco to the Piedmont, but the region proved better suited to grain and livestock. Expansive cattle

and horse farms have helped the region main-
tain its rural personality and open landscape
in the face of rapid population growth.

*On the horizon, Ashby's Gap opens the way for one of the major routes
from the Piedmont into the Shenandoah Valley.*

Virginia's New Frontier

✳ ✳ ✳

FOR MORE THAN A CENTURY AFTER CAPTAIN JOHN SMITH TURNED back from the river falls, the interior of Virginia still belonged to the Native Americans. They could not have guessed that the brief appearance of the English ships was the forerunner of massive white settlement and of the destruction of a culture little changed for centuries.

The Manahoacs and the Monacans, concentrated in villages near the Rappahannock and the James, traded and hunted with each other, gathered together for special occasions, and probably intermarried with other tribes scattered across the uplands toward the mountains. With the Powhatans in the Tidewater and with northern tribes who passed through on hunting and trading expeditions, they maintained a respectful distance and a generally effective peace.

The Indians encountered by the first English explorers understandably had not opened their arms to the visitors aboard the tall ships. To the first appearance of white men, their principal reaction was one of fear. A Manahoac detained by Smith managed to communicate the Indians' belief that the Europeans had "come from under the world" to take their land.

Years later, when English explorers pushed into the wilderness and set-tlers from the Tidewater began claiming pieces of the Piedmont, the fears the Indian had expressed to Smith were borne out. The Europeans did come to take the land, and the Manahoacs withdrew from the Rappahannock Valley. The tribe apparently had numbered no more than about 1,500, and it is now believed that they moved south and joined the Monacans, who lived in villages beyond the falls of the James. Experts have surmised that all of them moved on to the west, but it is unclear whether they left the Piedmont solely because of contacts with whites or whether the decisive pressure came from more aggressive northern tribes or an outbreak of disease.

In any case, it was neither the Manahoacs nor the Monacans who kept settlers from moving into the Piedmont. The physical challenge of surviving on a wilderness farm was formidable. Besides the struggle to produce food and endure the elements, there was both a psychological and physical threat from passing Iroquois hunting parties. The major hunting route used by the braves from the north crossed the Potomac into northern Loudoun County, passed the eastern flank of the Bull Run Mountains, crossed Cedar Run in southern Fauquier County, and forded the Rappahannock on the way to the James and hunting country beyond in North Carolina. There were other trails as well, and Iroquois parties often ranged far from them.

The Piedmont's first Europeans, therefore, settled within stockade walls near the river falls, where communities such as Fredericksburg would later take hold. These early settlers were less interested in establishing farms or villages than in trapping, exploring for minerals, and learning what lay beyond the mountains.

Out there in the distance, the Blue Ridge tantalized adventurers. Not far beyond the mountains, some thought, might actually lie the Indian Ocean that Christopher Columbus had sought. As early as 1653, colonial leaders considered an expedition to the Blue Ridge, but the idea was dropped, probably because the challenge was still too daunting.

Native American residents of the northern Piedmont, pressured by incursions of white men and aggressive hunting parties of northern tribes, moved away but left behind abundant evidence of their culture. Among the most common artifacts are arrowheads, such as this elegant example found at a ford on the Potomac.

In 1670, John Lederer, a young German physician recently arrived in Virginia, twice journeyed up river valleys searching for a mountain pass and a possible route to an East Indian sea. His second trip, commissioned by the colonial government, took him up the James to the mountain foothills, where he parted from his companions and, with an Indian guide, went on to the Roanoke Valley and then into North Carolina.

Several months later, Lederer led another party up the valley of the Rappahannock. Accompanied by John Catlett, a frontiersman and surveyor who had settled south of the river, and several other colonists, he reached "the top of the Apalataen [sic] Mountains" on August 16, 1670, perhaps near Swift Run Gap in Greene County. But he found no passage into the valley beyond.

Lederer was smitten with the country he crossed. Indeed, as he described it, some of the landscape must have looked like parts of Greene and Rappahannock Counties today, where cattle still outnumber people in secluded coves at the foot of the mountains.

After passing through forests along the Rapidan River, Lederer's party emerged into what he called open "savanae." "To heighten the beauty of these parts, the first springs of most of those great rivers which run into the Atlantick ocean or Chesapeack Bay do here break out and in various branches interlace the flowry meads whose luxurious herbage invites numerous herds of red deer to feed," Lederer wrote.

> The six and twentieth of August, we came to the mountains, where finding no horse-way up, we alighted and left our horses with two or

three Indians below whilst we went up afoot. The ascent was so steep, the cold so intense, and we so tired, that having much ado gained the top of one of the highest, we drank the King's health in Brandy, gave the mountain his name, and agreed to turn back again, having no encouragement for the prospect to proceed to a further discovery.

Lederer's accounts of his travels are somewhat suspect because they include obvious exaggeration and perhaps even outright fabrication. In reporting on his James Valley expedition, which took him into North Carolina, he told of spending twelve days crossing a barren, sandy desert. Such tales notwithstanding, there is no disputing the chief conclusion he drew from his trip up the Rappahannock Valley and on to the crest of the Blue Ridge. "They are certainly in great error," Lederer concluded, "who imagine that the continent of North America is but an eight or ten days journey over from the Atlantick to the Indian Ocean."

While the region still remained largely unexplored, Piedmont lands became an increasingly attractive investment for speculators and promoters. In 1688, entrepreneurs who had put together a 30,000-acre tract in present-day Fauquier and Prince William Counties established a fort near the Iroquois hunting trail. Their plan was to construct an enclosed town that would become a sanctuary for French Huguenots arriving from Europe in quest of religious freedom. Each family was to have a one-acre plot with a cabin inside the walls and a hundred-acre farm in the "country" outside.

Spring in the Blue Ridge brings a beautiful explosion of pink and white mountain laurel blooms. But thickets created by the shrub, also known as calico bush, spoonwood, and goose bush, are an irritant to hikers.

Although the threat from traveling Iroquois parties had abated, the dream of making this walled community of Brent Town into a vibrant frontier settlement failed. There were questions about boundaries, disagreements among owners of the land grants, and unanticipated delays. Finally, the tract was divided among the owners, and the plan was abandoned. More than a century later, a new community called Brentsville would be laid out on part of the tract, and it would be the fourth Prince William County seat.

✳ ✳ ✳

BY 1700, THE POPULATION OF THE VIRGINIA COLONY had grown to 58,000, and it was increasing at the rate of more than 20 percent each decade. Into the Piedmont rolled a wave of settlement, stimulated by the steady arrival of new immigrants from Europe, the deterioration of Tidewater soil repeatedly planted in tobacco, and the enticement of land speculators. The westward movement became a primary objective of the colonial government in Williamsburg during the administration of Alexander Spotswood, a combative and ambitious lieutenant governor.

Because the governor himself, the Earl of Orkney, chose not to cross the Atlantic and subject himself to the vicissitudes of life in the colony, Spotswood exercised the full powers of the office, dominating Virginia politics for twelve years. His service was marked by personal extravagance, feuds with the House of Burgesses in Williamsburg, and huge personal acquisitions of Piedmont land. At the same time, he moved forcefully to secure the frontier against the territorial ambitions of the French and to eliminate once and for all the intimidating presence of the Iroquois and their allies.

Cancelling a thousand-acre land grant limit, Spotswood opened opportunities for speculators and Tidewater aristocrats to enrich themselves on frontier property. He also laid plans for an arc of defensive outposts across the frontier, proposing to use friendly Indians to protect English settlers. In a meeting with leaders of the Nottoways, Saponis, and Tuscaroras, he offered to grant the tribes land for fortified villages and promised them exclusive hunting rights in the vicinity of the settlements.

On the Rapidan River, some thirty miles above the falls of the Rappahannock in present-day Orange County, he planned to locate a settlement of Tuscaroras who had moved into Virginia from North Carolina. The site was precisely where the main Iroquois hunting trail crossed the river.

As a further incentive, he offered to station a minister, a teacher, and a small military detail in the village and to send Englishmen regularly to trade for furs. Evidently, this was not enough for tribal leaders, for they led their people back to North Carolina.

Spotswood was undeterred. Rangers riding the frontier had reported finding silver and iron ore in the Rappahannock Valley, so the governor decided to establish a mining village at the site spurned by the Tuscaroras.

Conveniently, his friend Baron Christopher de Graffenreid had already arranged to bring nine German miners and their families to Virginia. When de Graffenreid ran short of funds, Spotswood took the opportunity to pay for the Germans' passage and put them into his personal service.

In the spring of 1714, the governor constructed his fortress with funds provided by the Virginia Assembly. Behind its walls, he settled the nine families, totaling forty-two men, women, and children, and named the place Germanna in honor of the residents' homeland and in tribute to Queen Anne. It was an important event in the opening of the Piedmont.

Beneath a fogbank near Fredericksburg, the Rappahannock River flows toward the Chesapeake Bay. Here Captain John Smith ended his excursion in 1608.

Although the Germans found recoverable ore in the area, it was two years before they started mining. In the interim, they subsisted by hunting, fishing, gardening, and raising pigs. Animal shelters were erected adjacent to the settlers' cabins, making for an unavoidably squalid existence.

After three years, the first settlers were joined by twenty more families from Germany. But unlike the first group, who had negotiated a contract of sorts with Spotswood, the new arrivals had come to Virginia involuntarily and were bound to the governor as indentured servants.

By the time the second group arrived, the original citizens of Germanna had come to feel blatantly victimized and had resolved to leave. Ignoring Spotswood's objections, they successfully applied for Virginia citizenship, which qualified them to receive land grants. In 1719, they moved away, settling twenty miles to the north, in what is now Fauquier County. There they founded a new community called Germantown, which quickly prospered. In a short time, the indentured servants also challenged Spotswood's authority and left. Some took up farming in present-day Madison County, others settled in Culpeper County, and some moved on to the Shenandoah Valley.

But the determined Spotswood had achieved his purpose. With the area secure, he doubled the size of his tract on the river, cleared forests, and established a furnace where iron ore was turned into ingots. As more settlers arrived, a new county was created and named Spotsylvania in the governor's honor. Germanna became its first county seat.

Although his encouragement of settlement and his steps to provide security on the frontier did much to open the Piedmont, Spotswood is best remembered as the first Englishman to reach the Shenandoah Valley. In 1716, when rangers discovered a passage over the Blue Ridge at Swift Run Gap, the governor quickly organized an expedition and personally led the first venture to stake England's claim to the land beyond the mountains.

With great fanfare, he departed the Governor's Palace at Williamsburg on August 20, waving to an excited crowd as he grandly rode away in his open carriage. At Germanna, he assembled a party of sixty-three horsemen, including rangers, Indian guides, and social friends accompanied by servants. Marching behind a trumpet and a pack of hounds, they set off into the wilderness, followed by a string of packhorses loaded with supplies, hunting gear, and an awesome quantity of liquor.

Spotswood clearly expected the trip to be an extended picnic, but he was soon surprised. On the way west, the explorers' fashionable clothes were shredded by thorns, and their horses were stampeded by hornets. Two members of the party came down with measles, and some turned back.

Germans who came to Virginia in the early eighteenth century as Governor Alexander
Spotswood's indentured servants later settled in Madison County. In the sanctuary of the
Hebron Lutheran Church near Madison, their descendants and descendants of other
German immigrants have worshipped since about 1740.

ABOVE AND OPPOSITE Salubria, a Georgian mansion near Culpeper, remains much as it was when it was constructed on the Virginia frontier in the mid-1700s. Built by the Reverend John Thompson, whose first wife was the widow of colonial governor Alexander Spotswood, it is believed to be the oldest brick house in Culpeper County.

On September 4, six days after leaving Germanna, they reached the crest of the Blue Ridge, where they drank toasts to all living members of the royal family, firing volleys into the air as they tossed down shots of brandy, rum, cider, champagne, wine, and a potent Irish liquor called usquebaugh.

The next morning, no doubt suffering from excruciating hangovers, they rode through the gap and down the western slope into the valley. There, they forded the Shenandoah River, claiming its west bank and everything beyond for King George I. After another raucous celebration, more grandiloquent toasts, a festive dinner of game, and a night's heavy sleep beside the river, Spotswood and his friends returned to Germanna, leaving a party of rangers behind to continue exploration of the valley.

Back in Williamsburg after the four-hundred-mile round-trip, the governor, much satisfied with himself, celebrated his feat by awarding each of his companions a memento in the form of a small golden horseshoe. Thus, they were immortalized as the Knights of the Golden Horseshoe.

The widely publicized exploit symbolically opened the way to a new frontier that had beckoned adventurers for decades. It emphatically announced the colonial government's intention to rule the land beyond the mountains and secure it from the French.

Spotswood missed the only discovery that would have excited him more than reaching the valley beyond the Blue Ridge—gold. There were small deposits not many miles from Germanna, but they were not discovered until years after the governor's death. It was not enough to launch a gold rush, but in the 1840s, Virginia would briefly send more gold to the U.S. mint than any other state. Most of it was panned from streams in Culpeper, Spotsylvania, Fauquier, and Orange Counties. After the California gold strike in 1848, however, prospecting gradually faded in the Piedmont, though there were recurring rumors of fabulous strikes. Today the Fauquier County community of Goldvein is one of the few reminders of the era.

The colonial governors who followed Spotswood made it increasingly attractive for new immigrants and old residents of the Tidewater to head west. Developers who had previously received land grants only when their settlers arrived in Virginia were allowed to claim land before they had arranged for families to occupy and farm it. Before leaving office, Spotswood himself took advantage of the land rush, acquiring a total of 83,000 acres of land south of the Rappahannock, including 40,000 acres when Spotsylvania County was organized.

When long-standing boundary questions were resolved, the boom spread north to the 6-million-acre domain of Thomas Lord Fairfax, which sprawled

In 1716, Alexander Spotswood and his famed "Knights of the Golden Horseshoe" crossed the Blue Ridge Mountains at Swift Run Gap and entered the Shenandoah Valley. In this view east from the valley, Swift Run Gap lies in the distance beyond Massanutten Mountain.

between the Rappahannock and the Potomac and reached across the Blue Ridge all the way to the headwaters of the Potomac and present-day West Virginia.

Since 1703 the land agent for this vast holding had been Robert "King" Carter, who had not acquired a single grant for himself in the Piedmont region. But now he obviously saw opportunity. In 1724, he obtained six tracts totaling 90,000 acres and shortly took another 52,000 acres in today's Fauquier and Loudoun Counties.

Six years later, Carter crossed the Blue Ridge to stake out 58,000 acres beyond Ashby's Gap. His friends enthusiastically followed his lead, acquiring similarly huge grants near his.

Beginning about 1725, settlers arrived in droves, clearing forests and building farmhouses, tobacco barns, and smokehouses from the timber and rocks found on the land. Farmers from the Tidewater brought with them slaves and tobacco plants. Germans and Quakers, moving down from the north, grew wheat and corn with remarkable efficiency and prospered without the use of slave labor.

Along the former Indian trails and roads leading toward Georgetown, Alexandria, Dumfries, Fredericksburg, and Richmond, taverns or "ordinaries" opened their doors to feed and shelter travelers, giving rise to the first communities.

The Red House, an ordinary on the Carolina Road, as the old Iroquois hunting path came to be called, was the beginning of the town of Haymarket. Around George Neavil's ordinary, where the route crossed a road from Dumfries to Winchester, the community of Auburn sprang up. Nathaniel Gordon's tavern, at an intersection where the Charlottesville-Fredericksburg road crossed a road from Richmond to the Blue Ridge, was the beginning of the town of Gordonsville. Leesburg's first houses rose around an ordinary owned by land developer Nicholas Minor.

The hamlet of Brandy Station got its start—and its name—from a tavern with a reputation for especially potent brandy. The tiny community of Boyd Tavern in Albemarle took its name from a colonial-era tavern on the Richmond-Charlottesville road. The settlement that became Fauquier Courthouse and later Warrenton started around a tavern at the intersection of the Winchester-Falmouth road and the Charlottesville-Alexandria post road.

Ordinaries provided more than food and shelter. They were de facto community centers whose owners purveyed gossip and political intelligence, brokered deals, and hosted public gatherings. Although licensed, they were of uneven quality—and reputation.

OPPOSITE Constructed in 1769 at the present-day community of Auburn in Fauquier County, Neavil's Mill today serves as the office of an architect. Through the eighteenth century, the mill and nearby ordinary operated by George Neavil served farmers and travelers going north and south on the Carolina Road and east and west on the Dumfries Road. George Washington was among the ordinary's guests.

✳ ✳ ✳

EARLY EIGHTEENTH-CENTURY PIEDMONT SETTLERS included families who would put their names not only upon real estate records and landmarks but on the Declaration of Independence and the Constitution of the United States, as well.

In 1723, Ambrose Madison settled on 5,000 acres in what would soon become Orange County. There, on the family's Montpelier estate, James Madison Jr., the fourth president of the United States, would grow up, live throughout his life, and die at the age of eighty-five.

In 1734, a well-connected farmer and mapmaker named Peter Jefferson claimed his first acreage on the Rivanna River, near a gap in Albemarle County's Southwest Mountains. There, his son Thomas would be born eight years later.

ABOVE   United States Chief Justice John Marshall was born in a log cabin, but in more prosperous times, Oak Hill, north of Salem, Virginia, became the family home. The town of Salem was later renamed in Marshall's honor.

OPPOSITE   The courthouse at Washington, Virginia.

In 1755, near the settlement of Germantown, Thomas and Mary Keith Marshall welcomed the first of their fifteen offspring and named him John. Forty-five years later, John Marshall would become Chief Justice of the United States Supreme Court and perhaps the most important interpreter of the Constitution in the nation's history.

Though born in the Tidewater region, George Washington made his mark on the Piedmont frontier as a teenaged surveyor for Lord Fairfax. In 1749, when he was but seventeen years old, Washington laid out the plan for a town in the Blue Ridge foothills, and Lord Fairfax promptly named it in his honor. Of the twenty-eight American towns named Washington, the one in Virginia was the first.

Later in his career as a surveyor, the future president became a prominent Piedmont landowner, buying nearly 3,000 acres between present-day Upperville and Paris as one of his many real estate investments.

The Madisons, Jeffersons, Randolphs, Lees, and Masons represented the Cavalier English who transplanted to the Piedmont some of the Tidewater social order, including slavery.

From Shadwell, Monticello, and Montpelier northward appeared new estates and splendid mansions with names such as Belmont, Exeter, Llangollen, Oatlands, Sully, and Raspberry Plain. They were attended by black servants, just as the stately manor houses of the Tidewater were.

For the most part, however, the region was settled by farmers who personally worked the land rather than planters who oversaw baronies worked by slaves. In addition to the immigrants from the Tidewater, the Piedmont received early settlers from the north. From Pennsylvania and beyond, covered wagons came down the Carolina Road, loaded with families of Germans, Quakers, and Scotch-Irish, who leased land for a few shillings per hundred

LEFT Two fireplaces in the great room of James Monroe's Oak Hill are graced by elegant mantelpieces presented to the President by General Lafayette, the French hero of the American Revolution.

ABOVE At Giles Fitzhugh's Weston estate, established in southern Fauquier County about 1753, servants did the cooking and other chores in this spacious summer kitchen. It is still maintained as it was in Fitzhugh's time.

acres per year. Craftsmen as well as farmers, the immigrants from the north fanned out into the Loudoun and Catoctin Valleys, built homes made of stones gathered from the fields, and created settlements such as Hillsboro, Lincoln, Lovettsville, and Waterford.

Settled by Pennsylvania Quakers in 1733, Waterford was for decades known as Milltown or Janney's Mill, in honor of its first settler. In addition to the mill itself, the village had a blacksmith forge, a cobbler shop, and a tannery. Its farmers tended some of the most productive fields in the Piedmont, growing a wide variety of crops and rotating them to renew the land.

Today old Waterford lives on beside Catoctin Creek, its history and architecture making it one of Virginia's most cherished places. Twenty-five years ago, the entire village was declared a National Historic Landmark because it had so faithfully maintained its eighteenth- and nineteenth-century ambience.

Amid the various Europeans in the eighteenth-century Piedmont lived hundreds of free African Americans—former slaves, former indentured servants who had completed their required servitude, and individuals of biracial parentage, born free because they had descended from a white mother.

ABOVE This wooden latch was fashioned by a skilled Quaker craftsman in the early eighteenth century. It continues to function on a closet door in a home at Lincoln, a Loudoun County village with Quaker origins.

OPPOSITE Now a residence, this is the second of three meetinghouses that have served the Society of Friends in Lincoln. Constructed about 1765, it served until 1815, when a new meetinghouse, still in use, was completed.

By 1800, the state counted 20,000 free blacks, and by 1810, the number had risen to 30,000. In spite of all odds, some of them prospered as craftsmen, artisans, and farmers. Outside Stevensburg, Willis Madden, whose mother had been an indentured servant on the Madison family's Montpelier estate, operated not only a farm, but also a tavern and campground for teamsters. Many whites were made uneasy by the increasing number of free blacks. In response, resolutions were introduced to prohibit African Americans from serving apprenticeships in trades and crafts and to require liberated blacks to leave the state within a year of gaining their freedom. The former provision was never enforced, and the latter was rejected by the assembly, but the existence of so many African Americans living free in a slave state created a political issue that grew until southern secession and the Civil War.

New Piedmont counties proliferated apace with settlement, usually spurred by farmers' complaints of being too far from their county seat. After

William Brown, a former parliamentarian of the United States House of Representatives, belongs to the eighth generation of his family to have lived at Oakland Green in Lincoln. Begun in the 1730s, the house is one of many historic homes in the Piedmont now operated as a bed-and-breakfast.

Spotsylvania County was created in 1721, Prince William followed in 1731. Orange was spun off from Spotsylvania in 1734. Orange begat Culpeper in 1748 and Greene in 1838. Culpeper was twice divided, creating Madison in 1793 and Rappahannock in 1833. Prince William was split to create Fairfax in 1742 and divided again to form Fauquier in 1759. Fairfax was broken up in 1757 to create Loudoun. Albemarle was established in 1744.

The new jurisdictions brought some order to life on the frontier, but few creature comforts. Even the well-to-do who could buy clothing, furnishings, and wine imported from England faced an arduous, isolated existence in Piedmont communities of the eighteenth and early nineteenth centuries. Local roads were hardly more than bridle paths that turned into mud bogs during the winter and spring.

Travelers seeking food and shelter at ordinaries often found accommodations abysmal. Mattresses were filled with straw or shucks, covered with sheets turned brown from use, and often infested with bedbugs. Strangers shared cramped, drafty rooms. Meals were indifferent or worse, typically consisting of bacon, eggs, and hoecake, washed down with peach brandy.

During the winter and spring, travel was a test of endurance, even on the most-used routes. No one knew that better than Thomas Jefferson, who made regular journeys to the Continental Congress in Philadelphia and to the new national capital on the Potomac. Although Jefferson sometimes stopped over

with the Madisons and other friends along the way, he became an expert on the taverns.

In an 1802 letter to a friend, Jefferson gave a pointed summary of the public houses along his preferred route, finding most of them acceptable: Wren's at Falls Church was "good," Brown's was "tolerable," Elk Run Church was a "pretty good house," Herring's was "clean and tolerably well," Stevensburg "will do," Orange was "a good house," as was Gordon's, but Bentivoglio's was "a miserable place." He was less charitable toward ordinaries in general. He advised his daughter, Martha, to take a good supply of food when she set out to visit him in Washington. "Cold victuals on the road," he told her, "will be better than anything which any of the country taverns will give you."

The perils of a journey across the Piedmont did not end with poor food and muddy roads.

Jefferson prudently carried a pistol, which he once lost, but apparently never had occasion to use. In 1807, in the midst of his second term as president, he very nearly lost his horse crossing the swollen Rapidan River. "My journey to this place was not as free from accident as usual," he wrote Martha after reaching the Executive Mansion. "I was near losing Castor in the

Rapidan by his lying down in the river, where waste [sic] deep, and being so embarrassed by the shafts of the carriage and harness that he was nearly drowned before the servants, jumping into the water, could lift his head out and cut him loose from the carriage."

For ordinary farmers on the frontier, travel was a rare experience. Life for them was a backbreaking and continuous struggle to wrest food, fiber, and shelter from the land. Livestock was so threatened by wolves that counties put bounties on them, paying off in tobacco when farmers turned in wolf heads.

Justice in Piedmont communities was often as harsh as the circumstances. Severe punishments were imposed for all manner of infractions, from cheating at cards and failing to attend church to stealing hogs. Penalties ranged from fines to be paid in tobacco to public lashings—and, for repeated hog thievery, hanging. For blacks, penalties were often more harsh. Their punishment for a variety of offenses was to have an ear nailed to a stake.

The harsh hand of the law did not eliminate criminal behavior. With Indians removed from the Carolina Road, sections of the route became the haunt of robbers and cattle thieves. For decades during the eighteenth century, a particularly notorious section near Auburn in Fauquier County was popularly known as Rogue's Road.

※ ※ ※

INDIAN TRAILS THAT SERVED AS MIGRATORY ROUTES for Piedmont settlers became the first farm-to-market roads linking the backcountry to river ports accessible to seagoing vessels.

These routes connected to new "rolling roads," created to enable farmers to roll huge barrels of tobacco, called hogsheads, to market behind teams of oxen. A pole inserted through the center of a filled hogshead served as an axle and effectively turned the barrel into a wheel. When new counties were created, officials were promptly besieged by requests for new roads. Often the task of construction fell to farmers who did the work without pay.

In the early years of Piedmont settlement, the colonial government encouraged farmers to grow tobacco. The towns of Alexandria and Dumfries, among others, got their starts with the establishment of government-supported warehouses. By the late eighteenth century, Fredericksburg had no fewer than eleven privately owned "rolling houses," and competition among them was fierce. But farmers on the frontier soon began to look for alternative crops.

Compared to Tidewater planters, Piedmont farmers owned few slaves. Moreover, their upland soil produced inferior leaves. Clearly, the crop that

OPPOSITE Although Montpelier has been modernized over the years, this rear colonnade remains as it was when President James Madison lived here. The estate was the home of the fourth chief executive from infancy until his death in 1836 at the age of eighty-five.

Located at the head of navigation on the Rappahannock, Fredericksburg was laid out in 1727 and developed into a thriving colonial port where tobacco was loaded aboard ships for export to England. A town of 4,000 by the Civil War, it was devastated by fighting in its streets in December, 1862.

had produced fabulous fortunes near the Chesapeake Bay and the lower Potomac would never make them rich.

These backwoods farmers observed Quakers, Germans, and Scotch-Irish farming without slave labor and succeeding by growing wheat, oats, barley, and corn. So began the inexorable transition from tobacco to grain and livestock farms. By the time of the Revolution, wheat was rapidly taking over tobacco fields, and the Virginia Piedmont formed the heart of the grain belt of America.

ABOVE AND OPPOSITE Dranesville Tavern, constructed about 1830, was a popular stopping place for Piedmont flour wagons on the road to Georgetown and Alexandria. It stands beside Leesburg Pike in western Fairfax County. Nearby ordinaries disappeared as wagon traffic waned, but Dranesville Tavern remained in business into the mid-twentieth century. Once near ruin, it was restored by the Fairfax County Park Authority, and is listed on the National Register of Historic Places.

As grain replaced the tobacco economy, roads to market were traveled by horse-drawn Conestoga wagons with shoulder-high wheels, loaded with wheat, corn, flour, or meal. A hundred-mile trip to Georgetown, Alexandria, Fredericksburg, or Richmond took upwards of a week.

On their return, wagons were loaded with supplies and provisions, including salt, cloth, plaster to be spread on the fields, and bushels of oysters to be sprinkled with salt and stored in cool cellars and spring houses.

Along heavily traveled roads, which have since evolved into U.S. Routes 29, 15, 7, and others, developed the eighteenth-century equivalent of interstate-highway truck stops. Taverns catering to the wagon trade offered pens, water, and hay for livestock, and food, coffee, liquor, and sleeping space on the floor for the drovers. They also provided valuable information. Tavern fronts were always papered with official notices, political news, circulars announcing lost animals and missing wives, and advertisements for horses, wagons, harnesses, and land for sale.

One of the busiest drovers' rests in northern Virginia was at Dranesville, an intersection of roads leading to Georgetown and Alexandria. It was a day's journey from the ports and a convenient stopping place. There, five ordinaries did business during the late eighteenth and early nineteenth centuries, with as many as forty to fifty wagons stopping overnight. Cattle, sheep, and even turkeys were herded into holding pens and daubed with color markings so that drovers could separate their property before hitting the road in the morning.

At strategic locations where roads converged with streams, large commercial grist mills converted grain into flour or meal, making transportation to market vastly more efficient. Their owners became brokers as well as millers, captains of the Piedmont's first industry.

Across the region, many of these mills remain. Some have been reduced to ruins, others stand defiantly against the ravages of the elements, vandals, and time—all monuments to the people who settled the wilderness. None has a richer history than Beverley Mill, beside Interstate 66 at Thoroughfare Gap in the Bull Run Mountains. It is said that this mill—which operated from the time George Washington surveyed the area and named the nearby peaks until Harry S. Truman was in the White House—sent flour to troops in five wars.

Rebuilt and expanded shortly before the Civil War, the millhouse was converted into a meatpacking house by the Confederate army. Herds of cattle and hogs were held in adjacent fields, and some two million pounds of beef and pork were put in storage in late 1861 and early 1862. When the army moved south in the spring of 1862, it set fire to the building to destroy the huge store of cured meat. Two years later, when the Union army moved out, the mill's machinery was wrecked and the building was torched once again.

When the Piedmont rose from the ashes years later, the mill was restored

ABOVE The interior of a typical Piedmont mill. Several across the region have been restored to working order.

OPPOSITE Regional mills created the first major industry of the Piedmont, converting wheat to flour for farmers from miles around. Rebuilt in 1856, Beverley Mill in Thoroughfare Gap operated from Colonial times until the mid-twentieth century. The route of Interstate 66 was changed to save the structure, but decades later it still awaits restoration.

to service. But by then, the heyday of the flour wagons and the great commercial mills of the Piedmont was past.

✻ ✻ ✻

IN THE EIGHT DECADES between the Revolution and the Civil War, the Piedmont ceased to be a frontier. Its natural wealth and the bounty of the Shenandoah Valley to the west stimulated monumentally ambitious river navigation projects, followed by a turnpike-building boom and the coming of the railroads—all supported by the merchants and shippers of Richmond, Fredericksburg, Falmouth, and Alexandria.

Even before the Revolution, George Washington had dreamed of linking the ports below the falls of the Potomac with the Ohio Valley. When the war was over, the general was enticed from brief retirement by Thomas Jefferson to organize the project. Between 1785 and 1799, the year Washington died, the Patomack Company invested $729,000 in locks and canals enabling barges to bypass raging falls above Georgetown. The system opened river traffic all the way to Cumberland, Maryland, where a proposed overland connection was supposed to link the Potomac to the headwaters of the Ohio.

First used in 1788, the canal moved $10 million worth of cargo (mostly flour, whiskey, and some furs) downriver to Georgetown before it went out of business in 1830. Its demise came because it could be used only during a relatively short period in the spring and fall, and because of plans to build the more efficient Chesapeake & Ohio Canal on the opposite side of the river.

Though widely considered a failure, the Patowmack Canal united the

contested western frontier with the fast-developing nation on the eastern
seaboard at a crucial moment in American history. And that had been
Jefferson's objective when he resurrected Washington's idea after the
Revolution.

At the same time that the Patowmack Canal was under construction, the
James River Company resumed work on locks and bypasses conceived and
started before the Revolution. They would serve for decades, making it possible for boats and barges to get past the rapids.

The canals on the Potomac and the James renewed long-standing aspira-
tions to open the upper Rappahannock to cargo traffic. Fredericksburg's port,
under intense competition from Richmond and Alexandria, was in decline. Its
merchants, and those across the river in Falmouth, were fighting to hold the

trade of Culpeper and Fauquier Counties. So in 1829, construction began on locks, dams, and canals to get boats past the rapids upstream from Fredericksburg. When work was finished in 1849, boats and barges loaded with two hundred barrels of flour could travel down to the port from fifty miles upstream and return with all manner of goods for farmers and merchants.

Unfortunately, by the time the canal was completed it was already obsolete. It never generated enough revenue to maintain its locks and dams, and within a decade it fell into bankruptcy and eventual ruin.

The project was doomed because the turnpike era had arrived full force, and new toll roads covered with stone and gravel now linked upcountry farms to Alexandria. Most prominent was the Little River Turnpike connecting the port city with the village of Aldie in Loudoun County. There, branches led to Warrenton, to Ashby's Gap, where U.S. Route 50 now crosses the Blue Ridge, and to Snicker's Gap, where U.S. Route 7 crosses the mountains. New roads also led west from Georgetown, from Fredericksburg, and from Richmond.

For a time, there was even a fascination with wooden roads. Having completed the Rappahannock Canal, the ever-competitive businessmen of Fredericksburg approved construction of a plank road to the town of Orange. The route was completed in 1853, but such roads quickly proved to be impractical. Subjected to Virginia's heat and wet weather, boards rotted faster than they could be replaced. In spite of such setbacks, privately owned turnpikes formed the beginning of the modern highway system.

By the 1840s, railroad tracks were being laid into Richmond, and soon construction began on the Orange and Alexandria Railroad running through Manassas Junction, Culpeper, and Gordonsville, with a spur track to Warrenton.

In 1851, the first rails were laid for the Manassas Gap Railroad. By 1854, rails connected Manassas Junction with Strasburg beyond the Shenandoah River. Although some leaders had initially viewed rails as mere feeders for the turnpike system, a new age had arrived. As surely as the Conestoga wagons had replaced oxen and rolling roads, the rails spelled the end of the spangled flour wagons and the professional drovers who gathered at Dranesville.

Like "ordinaries" all across the Piedmont, Buckland Tavern provided travelers welcome refuge from the elements in the early nineteenth century. Now a private residence, it stands beside heavily traveled U. S. Route 29 south of Gainesville, at the once vibrant milltown of Buckland.

Kenmore, one of the great eighteenth-century houses of northern Virginia, was the home of Fielding Lewis, a planter, patriot, and arms manufacturer who was married to George Washington's sister, Betty. Washington surveyed the property in 1772, and the house was constructed in 1776. A museum since 1922, it is furnished and maintained much as it was when the Lewis family was in residence.

Most of the Piedmont was spared from the fighting during the Revolution, but militiamen armed with skinning knives and squirrel guns were prepared for battle before the first shots of the war for independence were fired in Massachusetts. Revolutionary skirmishing and camp life are reenacted often on the Kenmore grounds.

Cradle of Democracy

✳ ✳ ✳

Before dawn on a spring morning in 1775, Virginia came to the brink of war against England and colonial rule.

After weeks of steadily rising tension, troops from a British schooner that was anchored in the James River slipped into Williamsburg while residents slept and carried away all of the colony's gunpowder, which was stored in the public magazine.

Word of the outrage at the Virginia capital swept through the Piedmont like wildfire, and out of the backwoods came militiamen armed with squirrel guns, tomahawks, and skinning knives. At Fredericksburg, their ranks swelled to nearly a thousand. Hundreds more assembled at Charlottesville and Orange, all of them ready to march off and recapture the barrels of powder. Bloodshed was averted only when George Washington and other prominent moderates in the Virginia Assembly sent assurances that the crisis could be resolved peacefully.

At the urging of the leaders, most of the angry farmers, merchants, and blacksmiths headed for home. The minutemen at Fredericksburg were dismissed. A column from Hanover County, led by Patrick Henry, was persuaded to turn back sixteen miles from Williamsburg. But companies from Charlottesville and Orange converged on the capital anyway, setting up camp and patrolling the village, where there remained an atmosphere of palpable tension.

Meanwhile, news reached Virginia that patriots in Massachusetts had met British troops with muskets at Lexington and Concord. The long fuse of rebellion had burned to an end. The first shots of revolution had been fired.

Six weeks after the raid on the magazine, Lord Dunmore, the colonial governor, fled Williamsburg under cover of darkness and established a command post aboard a ship anchored off the coast near Norfolk. In Philadelphia, the Continental Congress unanimously named George Washington as commander of the American army, and two weeks later Captain Daniel Morgan led the first company of Virginia troops north to join the general at Cambridge, Massachusetts.

The northern Virginia Piedmont would be spared much of the fighting in the long war for independence. But the region was in a real sense the spiri-

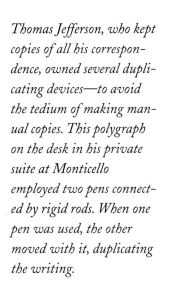

Thomas Jefferson, who kept copies of all his correspondence, owned several duplicating devices—to avoid the tedium of making manual copies. This polygraph on the desk in his private suite at Monticello employed two pens connected by rigid rods. When one pen was used, the other moved with it, duplicating the writing.

tual and intellectual wellspring for the Revolution and the creation of American democracy. Ideas spawned and nurtured on this picturesque Virginia frontier proved more explosive than the black gunpowder taken from the magazine at Williamsburg.

It was thirty-three-year-old Thomas Jefferson who finally distilled the purpose of the new nation in the ringing Declaration of Independence.

Responding to a resolution introduced by Virginia's Richard Henry Lee on June 7, 1776, the Continental Congress appointed a five-man committee to prepare a document declaring the colonies free and independent states. Because he was from Virginia, the largest of the thirteen colonies, and because of his much-admired writing skills, Jefferson was chosen to write the draft.

He composed the Declaration on a portable desk in his second-floor parlor in Philadelphia. Before him as he worked, he had a draft of a Virginia constitution he had just written. Jefferson, in fact, was not altogether happy at being in Philadelphia at that moment; he would have preferred to be back at Williamsburg where his friends were then completing the document for Virginia. He had sent his own draft to the convention, but it arrived too late to be considered. Now many of the ideas from that draft found their way into the Declaration for the new nation.

Before its approval by the drafting committee, Jefferson's work was reviewed by Benjamin Franklin and John Adams, who made only inconsequential changes. But when the full Congress debated it line by line, language blaming the King of England for the African slave trade was stricken. Jefferson was bitterly disappointed, but in his immortal preamble to the document signed on July 4, 1776, there remained the words containing the seeds of slavery's demise:

> We hold these truths to be self-evident, that all men are created equal, that they are endowed by their Creator with certain unalienable Rights, that among these are Life, Liberty, and the Pursuit of Happiness.

It was years before Jefferson was generally known to be the author of the United States' founding document. And it was also years before he took special pride in it. By then the Declaration, especially the preamble's stirring appeal to reason, was becoming recognized as one of the great documents of its time. Passing decades placed it among the momentous works of modern civilization.

Nearly two hundred years after the Revolution, historian Samuel Eliot Morison declared that America's war for independence would have been one of the world's defining events if it had produced nothing besides Jefferson's introductory words. The preamble, Morison observed, was "more revolutionary than anything written by Robespierre, Marx, or Lenin, more explosive than the atom, a continual challenge to ourselves, as well as an inspiration to the oppressed of all the world."

✳ ✳ ✳

WITHIN A LITTLE MORE THAN A GENERATION, one small corner of the world, the Virginia Piedmont, produced not only Jefferson, but James Madison, the chief architect of the American Constitution; George Mason, "father" of the Bill of Rights; Chief Justice John Marshall, who made the Supreme Court a binding force in American government; James Monroe, the president who led the new nation into world prominence; and George Washington himself. Though Washington and his neighbor Mason lived in the Tidewater section of eastern Fairfax County, they were fixtures of the culture that flowered on the Piedmont frontier and sustained the revolution.

All, with the exception of Marshall, who was born in a cabin and reared in homespun, were members of the landed gentry. And even Marshall was an aristocrat, for his mother was related to the Randolphs and a cousin of Thomas Jefferson. All had come from old Tidewater stock. Their families had been part of the migration to the Piedmont spurred by depletion of Tidewater

In 1822, Prince William County officials moved their offices into this courthouse at Brentsville, the fourth to serve the county since its creation ninety years earlier. In 1893, the county seat was moved to Manassas, and this old courthouse became a school and community center.

soil under the strain of repeated tobacco crops. Life on the frontier had imbued all of them with vigorous independence and self-reliance, and all had benefited from a far better than ordinary education for their time.

Washington, Mason, and Marshall had been educated at home. Jefferson and Monroe had studied at the College of William and Mary at Williamsburg, and Madison, after tutoring at home and instruction at a boarding school in the Tidewater, had gone north to the College of New Jersey at Princeton.

To varying degrees, all had been grounded in the classics, the natural sciences, philosophy, and religion. Thus prepared, they found debate and political discourse both satisfying and useful. Politics and government came to be their profession, their pastime, and their passion. Philosophical disagreement would eventually cause the cousins Jefferson and Marshall to despise each other and would create differences among Jefferson, Madison, and Monroe. There were few subjects upon which they all agreed. One, ironically, was slavery, for all considered the institution reprehensible and ultimately doomed, yet all held slaves of their own.

Gradually, these men became first dissidents, then activists, and, finally, revolutionaries.

For the leaders and political firebrands, and for many ordinary people of the Piedmont, the climactic event was the Boston Tea Party. Protesting a tax on imported tea, Massachusetts colonists had slipped aboard British ships and dumped 342 chests of tea into the harbor. Parliament retaliated with a series of "intolerable acts," as the colonists called them, including a blockade of Boston's port.

In Williamsburg, indignant Virginia burgesses brought outright revolution a big step closer. Adopting a resolution accusing Britain of a "hostile invasion," they so provoked Lord Dunmore that he dissolved the assembly. Eighty members, led by Patrick Henry, Richard Henry Lee, Jefferson, and Mason, promptly retired to the nearby Raleigh Tavern, where they drafted a message to all the other restive colonies. The communiqué, crackling with patriotic indignation, inspired the formation of the Continental Congress.

Across the Piedmont, citizens who had previously remained loyal to the crown now joined disgruntled neighbors in supporting the belligerent leaders in Williamsburg. In county after county, they voted to suspend all commercial dealings with Britain. Committees of Safety were established to impose punishment upon anyone who ignored the boycott against trade. Prince William County organized Virginia's first company of volunteer soldiers. Albemarle, Fairfax, Orange, Spotsylvania, and others promptly followed.

Among those transformed into patriotic zealots by the accelerating
events was James Madison, who had returned to the family's Montpelier
estate after his graduation from Princeton.

Long interested in the issue of religious freedom, Madison was outraged
when the colonial government jailed Baptist preachers in Culpeper County
for preaching without a license. As the Piedmont reacted to the blockade of
Boston Harbor, he became a member of Orange County's Committee of
Safety. He was also named a colonel in the county militia, organized by his
father, and became its procurer of arms and supplies.

In 1776, when Madison was only twenty-five, he became a member of
the Virginia Assembly, beginning a political career that would span four
decades and end with the presidency. His public service got off to an auspi-
cious start soon after his arrival in Williamsburg. There, throughout the summer, he worked on the Virginia constitution and George Mason's Declaration
of Rights, the precursor of the Bill of Rights appended to the U.S.
Constitution fifteen years later.

He also met Thomas Jefferson for the first time.

The author of the Declaration of Independence had resigned his seat in
Congress after approval of the Declaration and returned to Virginia to be

with his ailing wife. That autumn, Jefferson and Madison crossed paths in Williamsburg. Though they would not work closely together for another three years, their meeting in 1776 was the beginning of a personal, professional, and intellectual friendship that would continue until Jefferson's death, half a century later. During the course of it, they would exchange 1,250 letters, a correspondence that would become one of democracy's treasures.

✳ ✳ ✳

WITH THE OUTBREAK OF FIGHTING in Massachusetts and the flight of Lord Dunmore from the Governor's Palace in Williamsburg, the remaining Tory sentiment in the Piedmont collapsed. Only in Quaker communities, which were opposed to war on religious grounds, was there notable resistance to the struggle for independence.

ABOVE The prime weapon of the Revolutionary foot soldier.

OPPOSITE For seventeen years before her death in 1789, George Washington's widowed mother Mary lived in this Fredericksburg house, given to her by her son. She died after General Washington was elected first president of the United States, but before he was inaugurated.

As the first Virginia regiment marched north to join George Washington and local militias added every able-bodied man to their rolls, volunteers from Culpeper, Orange, and Fauquier Counties, including nineteen-year-old lieutenant John Marshall, drilled in a field near the Culpeper courthouse.

At Williamsburg, seventeen-year-old James Monroe, whose family had close ties to Washington, Jefferson, and Madison, helped organize a military unit at William and Mary. On the campus, students ablaze with patriotism protested alleged Tory sympathy in the school's administration and launched a raid on the Governor's Palace, capturing two hundred British muskets and three hundred swords, which they turned over to the local militia.

War finally exploded in the Old Dominion eight months after the shots at Lexington and Concord. At Great Bridge, the minutemen from Culpeper, joined by 250 regulars from North Carolina, decisively defeated a British regiment and captured a bridge and causeway controlling access to Norfolk. In thirty minutes of furious action, the redcoats saw nearly one hundred men killed, wounded, or captured, while one colonist suffered a minor wound.

Throughout the Revolution, other soldiers from the Piedmont would heroically distinguish themselves. It is not surprising that they did, for they were heirs to a growing military tradition. Their grandfathers had skirmished with Indian hunting parties, and their fathers had fought in the French and Indian War.

From 1776 to 1778, Virginia, the largest of the colonies, accounted for as much as one-third of the Continental army, raising fifteen regiments altogether. After the Battle of Great Bridge, boys and men from the Piedmont

STATESMAN
DIPLOMAT · AGRIST

WARRENTON
THE COURT HOUSE SETTLEMENT
WAS ESTABLISHED AS A MUNICIPALITY
UNDER THE NAME OF WARRENTON
JAN. 8, 1810, AND A SURVEY WAS
MADE MAY 6, 1811, BY WHICH SEVENTY
ONE ACRES WERE INCLUDED IN THE
TOWN LIMITS. WARRENTON WAS
INCORPORATED BY ACT OF ASSEMBLY
JAN. 14, 1819.

fought at Brandywine, Camden, Trenton, Guilford Courthouse, and Yorktown. But as the war dragged on and Washington's army suffered excruciating hardship, Virginia, like the other states, fell behind in its manpower commitments to the Continental ranks—notwithstanding extended enlistments, bounties for new recruits, and harsh action against deserters.

The shortage of men in the enlisted ranks was especially acute. In 1779, John Marshall, who had moved from the Culpeper minutemen into the Continental army after Great Bridge, came home because his regiment had been decimated by the expiration of enlistments. He waited in vain for a new command.

Marshall's boyhood friend, James Monroe, who crossed the Delaware with Washington in December 1776 and was later wounded in the Battle of Trenton, made two unsuccessful trips home to raise a new regiment. After failing a second time, he returned to civilian life and, at the age of twenty-one, took up the study of law under Jefferson, who became the decisive influence in his life.

To the farmers and villagers of northern Virginia, the war that once stirred such passion began to seem remote and unending. The largest enemy presence seen in the Piedmont during the entire struggle for independence was at a prison camp at Charlottesville.

Captured when British general John Burgoyne surrendered to Washington at Saratoga, three thousand prisoners were transferred to Virginia from confinement at Boston in the brutal winter of 1777-78. The prisoners, including Hessian officers with their wives and children, crossed the Potomac in rafts and boats threatened by floating ice, making their way south through a

For decades, travelers between Virginia and Maryland have crossed the Potomac on White's Ferry. A ford just downstream was a crucial river-crossing point during the Civil War.

half-frozen quagmire created by horses' hooves and wagon wheels.

They were almost out of food, but they received little sympathy from Virginians. The wife of Baron Frederick Adolph von Riedesel later recalled asking for food at a village, probably Auburn in Fauquier County, and being bitterly refused.

Once at Charlottesville with their new prison quarters completed, the captives enjoyed conditions better than those of Washington's army in the North. Prison rations were supplemented by vegetables grown by the prisoners themselves. Officers were allowed to rent quarters in the town. Baron von Riedesel and Major General William Phillips, the British commander of the contingent, even dined with Jefferson at Monticello.

Security at the compound was so lax that hundreds of prisoners simply walked away. Many of the Hessians made their way across the Blue Ridge, took up residence in German settlements of the Shenandoah Valley, married, and became American citizens.

By late 1780, the camp's population had declined by more than one-third. So, less than three years after it had suddenly become one of the larger population centers in Virginia, the camp was closed. British prisoners were marched to Frederick, Maryland; the remaining Germans were removed to Winchester, and eventually to Philadelphia.

✳ ✳ ✳

ONE OF THE REASONS for closing the Charlottesville prison was deepening concern that the war would come to the interior of Virginia. And indeed it did.

In December 1780, Benedict Arnold, the American traitor who had been put in command of a British task force, sailed down the coast from New York into the Chesapeake Bay. Without pausing, he proceeded up the James and attacked Richmond, which the legislature had made the new state capital.

Jefferson, who had succeeded Patrick Henry as governor, rushed his family to safety and hid the state's important records. But Arnold's arrival on January 5 created near panic in the town. The next day, the invading force of 1,700 men moved five miles upstream to Westham, where they burned a foundry, destroyed a magazine, and dumped gunpowder into a canal being excavated around the falls of the James. Arnold sailed back downstream and established winter quarters on the bay. The episode sent tremors through the Piedmont, for it was clear that there would be renewed threats in the spring.

Unbeknownst to residents of northern Virginia, the raid by the despised Arnold had very nearly been thwarted by one of their own, a strapping young sergeant major named John Champe.

The previous autumn, as Arnold was assembling a new regiment in New York, General Washington had devised a scheme to kidnap the turncoat officer, return him to the Continental army, and publicly hang him. For the ambitious assignment, he selected Champe, a member of the Virginia cavalry led by Major General Henry "Light-Horse Harry" Lee. A Loudoun County farmer before the war, Champe was an expert horseman and a crack marksman. More than that, he had impressed Lee as a man of extraordinary courage and determination.

Reenactors at Kenmore portray women who moved with army units and cooked for fighting men during the Revolution.

Under Washington's orders, Champe faked desertion from the Continental army camp at Tappan, New York, made his way to British lines, and joined Arnold's regiment on lower Manhattan Island. There the plot proceeded just as it had been designed by Washington, Lee, and Champe.

With the help of a civilian collaborator, Champe planned to overpower Arnold late one night when the general went into his garden to relieve himself before retiring. They would bind and gag him, then march him to a boat waiting on the riverbank. They would row across the Hudson to the New Jersey shore, where Lee's men would be waiting with fresh horses. Arnold would be locked up at Washington's headquarters before the British missed him.

In preparation, Champe secretly loosened boards in the fence around Arnold's garden, and his co-conspirator arranged for the rendezvous with Lee.

On the day before the abduction was to be carried out, Arnold's regiment was ordered, without advance notice, to board ship and sail for the Chesapeake. Unable to get away, Champe had no choice but to go with his unit. He was swept into the attack on Richmond and forced to spend the winter encamped with the redcoats near Portsmouth, maintaining his guise as a Continental army deserter.

In April 1781, Champe finally managed to escape and make his way south to the headquarters of General Nathanael Greene in North Carolina. He was eventually returned to Lee's command and revealed to his old comrades as a hero rather than a deserter. Concerned that Champe might fall into the hands of the British and be executed as a spy, Washington ordered him discharged from the army. With another spring at hand, the sergeant headed home to Loudoun County to put in a crop. After the war, he would briefly serve as sergeant-at-arms of the Continental Congress in Philadelphia.

✳ ✳ ✳

WITHIN DAYS OF CHAMPE'S ESCAPE from Arnold's regiment, the British once again moved toward the Piedmont. Having been defeated by Nathanael Greene at Guilford Courthouse in North Carolina, Lord Cornwallis opted to strike north into the Old Dominion as Arnold advanced up the James from the Chesapeake.

Once again, Virginia's state papers were removed from Richmond. And, in the face of superior enemy numbers, the Marquis de Lafayette, whom Washington had sent with 1,200 men to defend the capital, withdrew northward across the Rappahannock. With the city undefended, the legislature recessed on May 10, 1781, its members agreeing to reconvene in Charlottesville.

Presented with an inviting opening, Cornwallis saw the opportunity for a psychological tour de force even bolder than George Washington's plot to kidnap Arnold. The British would capture Governor Jefferson and the whole Virginia legislature.

But for the bravery of another Piedmont hero largely overlooked by history, the scheme might well have succeeded—with repercussions that are hard to imagine.

For the assignment, Cornwallis chose Colonel Banastre Tarleton, an officer especially hated and feared by the Americans. With 70 mounted infantrymen and 180 dragoons, Tarleton set out from Hanover County on a Sunday morning, planning to cover seventy miles in twenty-four hours. His strategy was to surprise the governor before he arose on Monday morning at Monticello and to simultaneously swoop down upon sleepy-eyed lawmakers in Charlottesville.

Fortunately for Jefferson, Virginia, and perhaps the Revolution itself, Tarleton's raiders were spotted on Sunday night by militia Captain Jack Jouett. They were then at Cuckoo Tavern, forty miles from their destination, but Jouett, the son of a Charlottesville tavern keeper, somehow discerned their objective.

Without being noticed by the redcoats, Jouett galloped off into the darkness ahead of them. Through the night, he spurred his horse across open fields and through the woods, hunching low in the saddle to dodge overhanging branches. It was just after dawn when he reached Monticello, where Jefferson was already at breakfast with his weekend guests, assembly speakers

ABOVE Some of the silver used at Monticello. Legend says that slaves hid it from British troops who came to the estate in an attempt to kidnap Jefferson.

OPPOSITE Although the dome atop Monticello helped to make Jefferson's home an architectural masterpiece, the room beneath it proved to be anything but practical. It was used as a playroom and storeroom during Jefferson's lifetime. Today it is closed to visitors because access is difficult.

Benjamin Harrison of the House of Delegates and Archibald Cary of the Senate. They were quite possibly discussing the selection of a new governor, for Jefferson's term had actually expired the previous Friday. The assembly had recessed, intending to take up the matter of a successor on Monday.

Jouett's warning of the approaching British was received without great alarm, and legend has it that Jefferson fortified the rider with old Madeira before the captain continued on to Charlottesville to alert lawmakers.

Had Tarleton not stopped along the way during the early morning hours, he might have succeeded in spite of Jouett. Once, his men interrupted their march to burn some American supply wagons they encountered. And just outside of town, they may also have paused for breakfast. Even so, Jefferson and the assemblymen got away without much time to spare.

After getting his family on the road, the governor took the time to collect some personal and official papers. Then, looking through a telescope into the village, he saw the British troops in the streets. As he departed, more of Tarleton's men were approaching the mansion.

In Charlottesville, seven legislators who dallied after receiving Jouett's warning were captured, but all the others, including well-known figures such as former governor Patrick Henry, escaped to Staunton in the Shenandoah Valley.

PAGES 94-95 Jefferson
was an enthusiastic and
scientific gardener. His
orchards, vegetable plots,
and vineyards were scenic
as well as productive.
Vegetables were produced
on a thousand-foot terrace
held by a retaining wall
and located on the south
side of the mountain to
gain full benefit of sunlight.

For his heroism, the twenty-seven-year-old captain was presented with a pair of fancy pistols. But his ride, at least as heroic as Paul Revere's six years earlier, was never immortalized in American folklore. The problem, historian Virginius Dabney lamented two centuries later, was that Jouett had no Henry Wadsworth Longfellow to turn his deeds into poetry.

The narrow escape from Charlottesville was one of the low points of the war in Virginia and of Jefferson's gubernatorial career. The author of the Declaration had been unhappy and much criticized during his two years as the state's second chief executive. In the debate preceding Thomas Nelson's selection as Jefferson's successor, some delegates even argued that the times required Virginia to entrust itself to a military dictator. Jefferson was scathingly criticized in the following weeks. Despite evidence to the contrary, political opponents accused him of cowardice during Benedict Arnold's January attack on Richmond and malfeasance in responding to the spring invasion.

But the end of the war was much nearer than it seemed during the gloomy interlude while the legislature took refuge beyond the Blue Ridge.

Several weeks later, General Anthony Wayne marched his Pennsylvania brigade down the Iroquois hunting trail to reinforce Lafayette and join with forces under Baron von Steuben. The British withdrew from Virginia's heartland.

By August, Cornwallis had moved his 7,000-man army to Yorktown. There he was trapped by a combined army of 9,000 Americans under George Washington and 7,000 Frenchmen led by Count Rochambeau. On October 19, 1781, the British commander surrendered. The war for independence was effectively over, though it would be more than a year before the definitive Treaty of Paris was signed and the British evacuated New York City.

✳ ✳ ✳

IN ITS INFANCY, THE NEW NATION was held loosely together by Articles of Confederation drafted by the Continental Congress in 1776. But after a decade, it was clear the states had to create a more purposeful union or risk disintegration and loss of the freedom the Revolution had won.

In April 1787, fifty-five delegates from the thirteen states convened at the State House in Philadelphia to write a constitution. Like the men who had fomented the war for independence, they were the country's establishment—lawyers, planters, judges, governors, former governors, members of the Continental Congress.

At his diplomatic post in Paris, Thomas Jefferson looked at the roster and admiringly observed that it was a convention of "demigods." First to

arrive—eleven days before the scheduled opening—was James Madison. At home in Virginia, he had been preparing for months, reading, writing, and corresponding with Jefferson and Washington. As he awaited the arrival of the other delegates, he put the finishing touches on a plan for the Constitution of the United States, fifteen resolutions creating a framework for debate and an outline for a new national government.

The bookish and retiring aristocrat from Orange County would emerge as the most influential figure in the creation of the U.S. Constitution. Through the weeks of debate, Madison put the fine points on the exquisitely sensitive issues of how to delegate and balance power in a new national government while preserving individual liberty and inalienable rights. It was he who kept the record of proceedings, spending hours each night transcribing his notes, and preserving the only firsthand account of the convention and the birth of the Constitution.

From Madison and the Virginia plan emerged the concepts of the two houses of Congress, an independent judiciary, and a "chief magistrate" to manage the affairs of the nation. Institutions were restrained by checks and balances intended to empower citizens.

From the outset, delegates favoring a strong national government looked to Madison and George Washington for leadership. The general, who was cheered by throngs of villagers as he made his way north from Mount Vernon, served as convention chairman. He spent little time in the presiding officer's chair and sat quietly in the Virginia delegation, but he exerted powerful influence behind the scenes.

Other Virginians strongly opposed Madison and Washington and insisted that all meaningful authority remain with the states. Patrick Henry refused to go to the convention at all. George Mason opposed the new Constitution because it contained no bill of rights. Governor Edmund Randolph refused to vote for it without a requirement for a follow-up convention for states to present amendments.

Madison brilliantly defended the document in the Federalist papers, published in the succeeding months, but it still faced fierce opposition in Virginia.

James Monroe, by now a Fredericksburg lawyer, and privately angry because he had not been named a delegate to the Philadelphia convention, joined efforts to block state ratification. But in June 1788, delegates to a convention in Richmond accepted the document by a vote of eighty-nine to seventy-nine.

It had become clear, however, that the American citizenry wanted a bill of rights. And three years later, it would be added in the form of ten amendments embracing essentially the same principles that George Mason had written into the Virginia constitution in 1776.

Tragically, the new Constitution did not come to grips with slavery. The issue already divided North and South. It was clear that southern states, Virginia included, would refuse to ratify a document that included a slavery ban, and they would be joined by other states where voters were lukewarm to a national constitution anyway. By omission, the remarkable blueprint invited destruction of the democratic government it established.

Three-quarters of a century later, the country, and especially the Piedmont, would pay a horrible price for ignoring Jefferson's preamble to the Declaration of Independence.

*At Ball's Bluff, near Leesburg, lies an unknown casualty
of the Civil War. Other unknowns, from both North and
South, rest all across northern Virginia.*

A Killing Ground

✻ ✻ ✻

W E WILL NEVER KNOW EXACTLY HOW MANY AMERICANS LOST their lives in the woods and fields of the Piedmont during the Civil War. The tragedy was so immense that it defied a complete accounting. Some of the victims were never found. Many were buried where they fell. Wounded often lingered for days, weeks, or months, and died after the war moved on. People simply disappeared.

Even now, 135 years in hindsight, the bloodshed across northern Virginia is breathtaking to contemplate. The best estimates: two battles at Manassas, some 30,000 killed, wounded, and missing. At Fredericksburg, 17,000; at Chancellorsville, 29,000; at the Wilderness, 30,000; and at Spotsylvania, 30,000 more. Thousands of them were Virginians. Some were only boys, killed on the fields they had recently hunted and plowed.

From victories in the Piedmont, Robert E. Lee launched his two drives into the North, ending at Antietam and Gettysburg; to the Piedmont he returned to pull his mangled army back together. In the Piedmont, the corridor to Richmond, Union forces suffered their deepest frustrations and most bitter defeats before Ulysses S. Grant led them on to the siege of Petersburg and victory at Appomattox.

Living off the land, the armies left it—sometimes unavoidably, sometimes by design—ravaged. When the soldiers clashed, the violence produced grotesque spectacles against the pastoral backdrop: dead men and horses, splintered trees, wrecked wagons, and disfigured survivors. More than fifty years after the Battle of First Manassas, Marianne E. Compton, a local woman, vividly recalled what it was like at her home when the nearby fighting stopped:

> The yard paling was gone . . . used to make fires. Soldiers, our southern troops, were everywhere, in stables, barns, and smaller outhouses. All the lower part of the house was filled with wounded. We walked through a lane of ghastly horrors on our way upstairs. Amputated legs and arms seemed everywhere. We saw a foot that had just been cut off lying on one of our dinner plates. . . . One of the first wounded men brought into this temporary hospital was a most interesting young officer, Henry W. White of the Washington Artillery, Louisiana. He bled to death in our parlor and was buried under a large walnut tree on the lawn. There his remains still lie, surrounded by a stone wall.

Year after year, decisive moments of the Civil War are reenacted with sound, fury, and devotion to history. This thunderous recreation of an engagement at Manassas took place not on the battlefield, but on private property. The battlefield itself—the site of two monumental struggles—is now a national park.

Today, most Americans know the war in Virginia through the epic battles at places seared into the national conscience: Manassas, Fredericksburg, and Chancellorsville. On these old battlefields and others where pivotal engagements were fought, the fallen are memorialized in serene military parks adorned with monuments, split-rail fences, spiked cannons, and simple tombstones. The hushed killing grounds are mapped for self-guided tours and preserved more or less as they were when armies met. Hundreds of thousands of visitors come each year, generation after generation, to see where, learn how, and contemplate why ancestors died.

But all across the Piedmont lies other hallowed ground. In one way or another, every town and crossroads was swept into the conflict and paid its own price. Every Piedmont county has its own monuments, its own stories of tragedy, its own historic moments.

At Delaplane, then called Piedmont Station, Colonel Thomas J. Jackson put his brigade aboard freight cars on the Manassas Gap Railroad and rode to immortality at the Battle of First Manassas. On Ball's Bluff, not far from Leesburg, Confederate defenders met Union raiders in hand-to-hand combat and drove them into the Potomac, where the more unfortunate died desperately trying to swim to safety.

Near Catlett Station, Lieutenant George Armstrong Custer won a little-noticed skirmish in early 1862, marking the first victory of a flamboyant military career best remembered for its ending, years later and far away, at the Little Bighorn.

At Rectortown, Major General George B. McClellan, having proved himself no match for Robert E. Lee, was fired by Abraham Lincoln as commander of the Union's Army of the Potomac.

In swirling dust at Brandy Station, horsemen armed with flashing sabres and blazing revolvers fought the largest cavalry engagement of the war. Confederates won the battle, but lost forever their vaunted image of invincibility.

At Aldie, more than a hundred Virginians in J.E.B. Stuart's cavalry were killed or wounded fighting around haystacks, through gullies, and over stone walls along the Little River and Snickersville Turnpikes.

At Waterford and elsewhere, passions fired by the issues of slavery and loyalty caused neighbors, family, friends, and brothers to take up arms against each other.

And at farmhouses scattered from the Bull Run Mountains to the Blue Ridge, residents provided hideouts for John Singleton Mosby's Confederate rangers, who created havoc behind Union lines, dominating a twenty-square-

Union dead at Ball's Bluff are buried in the nation's smallest national cemetery. Coming soon after the Confederate victory at the Battle of First Manassas, the Union debacle at Ball's Bluff created an uproar in Washington.

ABOVE Fauquier County in full bloom, viewed from Wildcat Mountain. Unspoiled land-scapes such as this one have provided continuity across generations of northern Virginians. Their future weighs heavily upon land-use planners.

OPPOSITE A silent sentinel at Manassas.

mile swatch of Fauquier and Loudoun Counties known as "Mosby's Confederacy." For the last two years of the war, the "Gray Ghost" and his men plagued the Union army, kidnapping officers, wrecking railroads, looting supply shipments, and confiscating horses, mules, and weapons by the thousands.

Names of places have been changed and landmarks have disappeared, but ghosts and scars of the war endure across the resilient land. Stone fences chipped by minié balls and stained by blood still stand. Backroads traveled by Mosby's men remain unpaved, and flames flicker yet in fireplaces where he and his rangers thawed themselves and dried their soggy clothes after raids on winter nights.

Soldiers who passed through the Piedmont between 1861 and 1865 could still get their bearings if they returned today to the region whose natural beauty impressed them even in wartime. "This country is so beautiful, I wish I had been born here," a Connecticut corporal wrote after arriving in northern Virginia early in the war. To some, including Union General John Pope, Rappahannock County was reminiscent of Switzerland.

For Piedmont towns and those who lived in them, the war quickly became a struggle for survival—just as it was for the soldiers who fought around them.

Fredericksburg changed hands seven times during the course of the war, and battles twice swept through its streets. Nearly every house left standing after the first battle in December 1862 had been damaged by artillery or minié balls, and many of them had been looted and left open, their furniture thrown into the streets.

Counties spared destruction by combat suffered nevertheless.

In 1862, the U.S. Congress adopted harsh measures to deal with secessionists. Virginians who declined to pledge their loyalty to the Union could be expelled from federally occupied territory and regarded as spies if they returned. Their property could be, and sometimes was, seized without compensation.

Given explicit authority to gather food from the territory they occupied, Union army troops lived off the land, exacting a painful toll during the spring and summer of '62. North of the Rappahannock, they looted orchards, cellars, smokehouses, and barns. Fields were stripped, gristmills were wrecked, livestock was driven away. Union encampments became slaughter pens for Virginians' cattle, hogs, and sheep, and overnight, families of means found themselves destitute.

The behavior of occupying forces chilled Piedmont inhabitants. In a letter to her husband in Richmond, Susan Jeffords Caldwell of Warrenton related how Pennsylvania troops were implementing the confiscation policy mandated by Congress:

> Mrs. Fairbanks, a lady from Baltimore who occupies Mrs. Shackleford's house, has been ordered to move out, and give up the house to a Capt. for the accommodation of his family. She asked permission to retain two rooms, and it was coldly granted—they have taken possession of everything belonging to Mrs. Shackleford—even to the cooking stove—use all the vegetables from the garden themselves—say it is Rebel property and it belongs to them since the confiscation bill was passed. I understand they have taken Rice Payne's house as the Head Quarters of the General—and Dr. Bacon's seminary as a Hospital—they have turned their mules into Dr. Bacon's garden. Mrs. Fant's and all the lots are now filled with their horses and mules—our land will be laid waste and we have no hope of a crop for the coming season. Keith's factory was burned yesterday—and every barrel of flour taken from John White—and the mill dam opened to allow the water to run in—the destruction of property is awful to think on and have it to realize [sic] they destroy as they march on—even stone fences are destroyed. . . .

> You would scarcely recognize our town—streets are filled with soldiers—and every little shantee filled with goods brought up by the dutch and all kinds of yankeedom. Most of our stores are closed. . . . The Stars and Stripes are flying from the Court House—hard indeed is it for us to bear with any degree of patience. Very seldom are ladies seen on the streets, only on very urgent business . . . to look out one would suppose we would never have our town again in our possession.

Far from the major battlefields, firefights constantly erupted, especially in areas where partisans farmed by day and fought by night. John Divine, a Leesburg Civil War buff and historian, has spent years examining the skirmishes fought across Loudoun County. "I don't believe there was ever a day during the Civil War without shots fired in anger in this county," he says, "not one."

Like the rest of the Piedmont, Loudoun County was generally behind the Confederate cause, but in communities such as Lincoln and Waterford, most of the inhabitants were opposed to slavery and opposed to secession. In the state secession referendum, Waterford residents voted 221 to 36 against

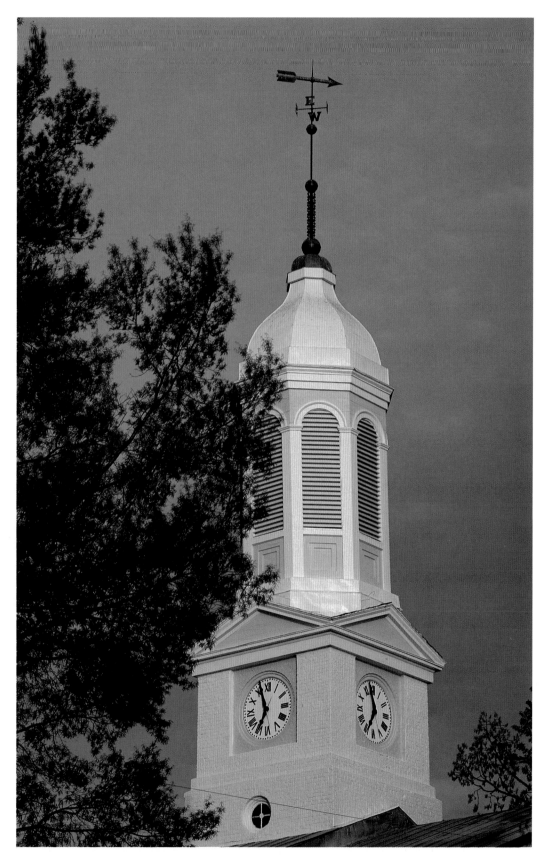

Warrenton's most prominent landmark, the bell tower of
the Fauquier County courthouse.

Traffic no longer crosses the Goose Creek Bridge, a masterpiece of stone masonry left isolated beside modern U. S. Highway 50 near Atoka. During the Civil War, it was a landmark on the Ashby Gap Turnpike, a road that served as the boulevard of "Mosby's Confederacy."

leaving the Union, and most of its inhabitants remained fiercely loyal to the government in Washington. Waterford miller Samuel C. Means, whose home still stands in the village, raised a cavalry company, the Loudoun Rangers, and carried out hit-and-run warfare against Confederates—much as John Mosby did against federal troops. It was the only organized unit of Virginians to fight on the side of the Union during the war.

On August 26, 1862, Means's company arrived in Waterford and occupied the Baptist church, using it as headquarters for scouts sent into the surrounding countryside. Before dawn the next day, while Means was at home visiting with his family, the church was attacked by a company of the Virginia cavalry's 35th Battalion, an outfit composed of men from Loudoun County. For three hours, Means's troopers returned the fire that spattered off the church walls and pierced its windows.

Twice a cease-fire was called, and Mrs. Henry Virts, a brave woman who lived nearby, went into the church to deliver a Confederate demand for surrender. But not until Means's men were running out of ammunition did they surrender to Captain Elijah White, who had been a local farmer before the war.

Each side had seen one man shot dead and several others wounded. The church sanctuary, where bleeding soldiers lay in pews, had the look of a slaughterhouse. In most respects, it had been a rather ordinary skirmish, but it revealed personal hatred and bitterness in an area where loyalist sentiment was strong. On this August morning in Waterford, Charles Snoots had been among the defenders inside the Baptist church, and his brother William had been among the attacking graycoats outside. As the Union company was disarmed, William Snoots made a final attempt to shoot his own brother, and would have succeeded but for the intercession of a Confederate officer.

Just as it was elsewhere, the Civil War in the Piedmont was remarkable for its brutality and hardship. Here fathers searched among the dead for the bodies of their sons, survivors returned to fight new battles over the shallow graves of fallen comrades, soldiers dressed in rags marched on bloody feet, fought on empty stomachs, survived, arose, and fought again.

There were moments, wrote the historian James McPherson, when men were thrown into a "superadrenalized fury that turned them into mindless killing machines heedless of the normal instinct for self-preservation."

It was also a war with moments when humanity, nearly snuffed out by the organized savagery, spontaneously flickered. There were cease-fires to allow hungry soldiers from both sides to pick blackberries in a no-man's-land between them; touching reunions of former West Point classmates while battlefields were cleared of the dead and wounded; love affairs between frightened Union boys and lonely southern girls; low conversations between Union and Confederate pickets on opposite sides of the dark Rappahannock.

After the war was over, Union Lieutenant George Round would return to Manassas and lead a massive tree-planting campaign, beginning the area's recovery from devastation.

✳ ✳ ✳

ON MAY 24, 1861, the morning after the referendum that took Virginia out of the Union, the killing began. Led by Colonel Elmer E. Ellsworth, a friend of President Lincoln's, New York Zouaves crossed the Potomac from Washington to occupy Alexandria. From the waterfront, the colonel led a column up King Street to Marshall House. The four-story hotel and tavern flew a large Confederate flag, visible to Lincoln through his telescope in the White House. Mounting the stairs, Ellsworth personally struck the banner, but as he descended to the street, his way was blocked by one James W. Jackson, who stepped out of a room with a double-barreled shotgun. Before Ellsworth could react, he was shot in the chest and killed. A Union infantryman shot Jackson and killed him as well.

Ellsworth was perhaps the first Civil War casualty on Virginia soil—if one discounts the

The Loudoun County Courthouse at Leesburg, like so many across Virginia and the South, pays tribute to fallen Confederates.

twenty-one men who died in 1859 as a result of John Brown's raid on Harpers Ferry. The New York colonel was also the Union's first hero, a symbol immediately used to whip up war support in the North.

Huge crowds streamed past his casket as he lay in state at the Washington Navy Yard. A funeral service was held for him at the White House, and for years to come, Marshall House would remain a shrine to Union loyalists.

For two months after Ellsworth fell, northerners told themselves the secessionist uprising would be short-lived. The Union army would march to Richmond and end it, and all the boys would go home. That delusion was shattered by the stunning Confederate victory at Manassas in July. The battle left the Rebel army in possession of a strategically important railroad intersection controlling access to the heart of Virginia.

ABOVE *Members of the 84th New York Volunteer Infantry, also known as the 14th Brooklyn, fought bravely in both of the epic battles at Manassas. They are memorialized by a monument on a ridge where they met Major General John B. Hood's division of Texans on August 29, 1862.*

OPPOSITE *An unabashedly romanticized 1938 rendering of General Thomas J. Jackson stands on the crest of Henry House Hill at Manassas. Here Jackson and his brigade of Virginians turned back a furious Union charge on July 21, 1861.*

From that first major engagement of the war came some of the most
vivid images of the entire struggle.

Soft and unsuspecting Union troops discarded clothing and equipment
and broke ranks to pick berries as they made their way to Manassas Junction
in the heat. Finding themselves in a furious battle, they fought bravely, and it
seemed for a time that they had won. But in a decisive struggle for the sum-
mit of Henry House Hill, Virginians led by Colonel Thomas J. Jackson
turned back their assault, earning Jackson the sobriquet "Stonewall." The sub-
sequent withdrawal of General Irvin McDowell's troops across nearby Bull
Run disintegrated into a humiliating rout and then a pell-mell flight back to
Washington.

The disorganized federal troops were joined by carriages filled with
panic-stricken sightseers, including members of Congress, who had come out
with parasols and picnic baskets to watch the battle from open hillsides.

Soldiers cut mules loose from supply wagons, jumped on their backs, and
rode away, dragging harnesses behind them. Carriages were wrecked, supplies
were dumped, and wounded were left behind. Mathew Brady, the portrait
photographer, who had arrived from Washington with two wagonloads of
equipment to photograph the battle, had his chemicals spilled and his plates

broken, and wound up lost in the woods overnight. He returned to Washington with few pictures of the bitter fight preceding the rout and no images of the army's ignominious scramble back to the capital.

The disaster at Manassas had a powerful and strengthening effect in the North. The struggle on the banks of Bull Run had destroyed the presumption that the conflict would be brief and that its outcome was ordained. Across the South, the news from Manassas produced ecstasy, but inhabitants of the Piedmont were sobered by a close view of war's ghastly consequences.

Eighty-year-old Judith Henry, a widow whose farm was at the center of the fighting, was mortally wounded in her bed when cannon shot penetrated the walls of her house. The next day, as the dead soldiers were being taken from the battlefield, Mrs. Henry was laid to rest. Nanny Neville Leachman Carroll, a young neighbor girl at the time, later recalled:

> Early on the morning after the battle, young Mr. Henry, from Henry House, came over, saying his mother had been wounded seven times in her bed during the battle, and had died in the night. He asked if Mama and Granty would return with him to prepare her body for burial. Of course they went and stayed `til he, with the help of a neighbor, had buried her. They had gone a short cut across the fields, about a mile, and found the going difficult because of the dead soldiers everywhere. Returning they came by the road, and it was much worse.

Eight months passed before the Army of the Potomac was ready for another drive on Richmond.

ABOVE Mrs. Judith Henry was fatally wounded while lying in her bed as fighting raged around her home during the Battle of First Manassas. When the war ended, the house had been reduced to rubble and ashes. Family members rebuilt on the same site.

OPPOSITE During the Battle of First Manassas, this old stone bridge across Bull Run provided an avenue to and from the battlefield. It was destroyed by the withdrawing Confederate army the following spring and rebuilt in the 1880s.

Manassas Junction, a railroad intersection providing
access to the heart of
Virginia, made the lush
Prince William County
countryside strategic
ground in the Civil War.
In scarcely more than a
year, two epic battles were
fought across it, both ending in victory for the
Confederacy. When the war
was over, the landscape was
barren.

President Lincoln preferred an attack on the 45,000-man Confederate army of General Joseph E. Johnston, which had wintered around Manassas and Centreville, but Major General George McClellan opted to send his 100,000-man army down the Potomac on ships and barges to attack the Confederate capital from the southeast. After two months of fits and starts and pressure from Washington, McClellan advanced up the peninsula to the outskirts of the city and prepared to lay siege to it, but Robert E. Lee's defenders drove Union forces back and turned to attack General John Pope's army strung out along the Rappahannock.

In August, Lee trapped Pope at Manassas. The ensuing battle, the second on the plain of Prince William County in a little more than a year, ended with the Union army again driven back to Washington. Lee promptly crossed the Potomac into Maryland and Union territory.

Days later, in the Battle of Antietam, the Army of Northern Virginia suffered more than 10,000 casualties in a single bloody day before Lee led it back across the Potomac to Virginia. At Fredericksburg that December another Union drive toward Richmond was crushed.

In the spring of 1863, in what many historians and military analysts regard as the tactical masterpiece of the war, Lee defeated a Union army led by Joe Hooker at Chancellorsville, setting the stage for his fateful march into Pennsylvania. His defeat at Gettysburg, coupled with the loss of Vicksburg to Ulysses S. Grant, effectively sealed the Confederacy's fate.

The fighting across the Piedmont would be forever remembered—for stunning tactical genius, for perseverance in the face of grinding hardship, and for heroism on a monumental scale. It was exemplified at Second Manassas, where Confederates who had exhausted their ammunition defiantly stood their ground, hurling rocks at onrushing New Yorkers.

At Fredericksburg, wave after wave of Union troops advanced into the muzzles of Lee's dug-in army and fell into piles like cordwood. At the Wilderness, wounded from North and South died together as fire swept through the tangled undergrowth around their trenches. Hundreds of dead were left on the battlefield unburied when the armies moved a few miles to Spotsylvania and again hurled themselves into the face of muskets and cannons.

Nearly always outnumbered, Lee made brilliant use of the Piedmont terrain, taking refuge behind the Rappahannock and the Rapidan, hiding crucial troop movements behind the mountains, keeping himself between Union forces and Richmond. At crucial moments, he took gambles that invited destruction of his army. Before the Battle of Second Manassas and at Chancellorsville, he divided his forces in the face of superior enemy numbers for flanking maneuvers that brought him victory and made him a legend in the North as well as the South.

Confronting John Pope's army along the Rappahannock in August 1862, Lee sent Stonewall Jackson's "foot cavalry" on a grueling march covering fifty miles in just two days in order to get behind Pope and strike from the rear. West of the Bull Run Mountains, Union cavalry saw Jackson's corps of 24,000 moving northward, leading Pope to conclude that the Confederates were heading for the Shenandoah Valley. But after a brief rest at Salem, which is now the town of Marshall, Jackson turned east and passed unmolested through Thoroughfare Gap, behind the Union army.

In his diary, Edward Carter Turner, a well-to-do farmer whose Kinloch estate lay just west of the gap, described the passing of Jackson's Corps:

> All day long our house and yard are filled with soldiers, hungry, thirsty, barefooted, and some of them almost naked, but bright and buoyant, asking only a mouthful to eat and to be led against the enemy. The people everywhere relieve them to the utmost of their ability, but having been severely plundered by the Feds., little and in many instances nothing is left to feast them on. They take gratefully, however, whatever is

OPPOSITE On the day after the Battle of First Manassas, Judith Henry was laid to rest in the family plot near her shattered home.

Chatham Manor, overlooking the north bank of the Rappahannock, opposite Fredericksburg, served as headquarters for Union forces during their attack on the town. On Chatham's lawn years earlier, the young Robert E. Lee had courted Mary Custis, his bride-to-be.

Across the river from Chatham Manor, Lee made his headquarters at Brompton House on Marye's Heights. Later in the war, the Union used the house as a hospital for wounded from Spotsylvania. It is now the Mary Washington College president's residence.

given and go on rejoicing in the prospect of speedily driving the enemy from their soil and the return of sweet peace. Among those who arrive for a scanty meal are our two sons Tom and Beverley, our nephew Wilson and several of our Randolph cousins.

In spite of its condition, Jackson's corps pressed on. That night, August 26, the weary troops wrecked the vital Orange and Manassas Railroad at Bristoe Station and destroyed the huge Union supply base at Manassas Junction to begin the battle. By the time Union forces realized what had happened and rushed to block Thoroughfare Gap, their response was too little and too late.

Two days behind Jackson, General James Longstreet's corps, accompanied by Lee, fought its way through the gap, clearing Union defenders from the rugged flanks of Leathercoat Mountain to reunite the Army of Northern Virginia and bring the Confederacy a second huge victory at Manassas.

ABOVE A Manassas fire-fight reenacted.

OPPOSITE Erected in 1848, the Stone House on the Manassas battlefield served as a tavern and as a farmhouse before the war swept through in 1861. During the two battles around it, the house was pressed into service as a hospital and as a Union headquarters.

His army safely through the opening in the mountains, Lee dined and spent the night at Avenel, a plantation just west of the gap owned by Robert Beverley, whose wife was the general's cousin. Many years later, Mrs. Beverley would recall the quiet evening before the battle.

At dinner, Lee and his aides were served warm milk "just from the cow" because all the chilled milk had been given to hungry soldiers passing during the day. Members of the general's staff slept on pallets spread on the floor. "At supper, he [Lee] was the life of the whole crowd and kept everyone laughing and in good spirits," Mrs. Beverley recalled.

> That night, he slept in the little room and members of his staff slept in the room at the head of the stairs and in the far room. The servants were up nearly all night cooking breakfast for the staff, which, of course, left early. I did not come out in the morning, but from the end of the porch, I saw the General mount his gray horse and at the head of his staff ride down the road at the foot of the garden. They told me he had been heard walking the floor until 3 o'clock in the morning. . . .

Lee's boldness and tactical wizardry notwithstanding, the Confederacy was doomed to lose the war. The Union had too many men and its army was

ABOVE Built by Revolutionary War hero William Champe Carter, the Farley mansion at Brandy Station served as the headquarters of Confederate cavalry leader J. E. B. Stuart and as a hospital during the Civil War's greatest cavalry engagement. It was later pressed into service as a headquarters by the Army of the Potomac.

LEFT Welfords Ford Road, an important north–south route during the Civil War, was traveled by Stonewall Jackson's corps on the way to the Battle of Second Manassas. Robert E. Lee and James Longstreet used it on their way north to Gettysburg. This segment in the Brandy Station battlefield has changed little over the decades. Like some other historic backroads, it remains unpaved.

too well equipped. Confederate fighting forces had to live largely off the land, and by the second year of the conflict much of the land was barren. Union officers commanding occupying forces in the Piedmont complained that it was difficult for their troops to find sufficient food. Some areas, such as the gentle plain around Manassas Junction, resembled a moonscape. After two enormous battles, the only thing left standing at Manassas was Liberia, the estate of William J. Wier, a house which within a year had hosted both Abraham Lincoln and Jefferson Davis with their respective generals.

Had the area been able to sustain life, there might have been a third Battle of Manassas in the fall of 1863. But Lee concluded that the country-side could no longer provide for an army. Fences were down, livestock was gone, and instead of wheat or corn, the fields were covered by waist-high weeds. Where stands of hardwoods had grown nothing was left but stumps.

The nearby town of Haymarket had been put to the torch by Union soldiers, leaving only three houses standing among forlorn chimneys that rose above blackened ruins.

St. Paul's Church, used as a hospital and finally as a stable for Union cavalry horses, survived all of the fighting, but it, too, was finally burned by retreating federal troops, leaving only its walls. In its shadow were three mass graves, one with the bodies of eighty Confederate soldiers who died at First Manassas, another with Union men from Second Manassas, and a third with members of the 11th Alabama regiment, who had died in a measles epidemic in 1861.

For the northern Piedmont and all of its people, the burden of Union occupation had become increasingly heavy with every passing month. Within the first year of the war, food prices doubled. There were shortages of nearly everything, especially coffee, sugar, and flour. By 1863, a barrel of flour cost three hundred dollars, a bushel of corn meal ten dollars. To deal with the critical shortage of salt, county officials designated special salt commissioners who endeavored to buy supplies in bulk and control their distribution. In the countryside, some desperate families boiled the boards from their smokehouse floors to recover brine. For lack of salt, livestock died on some of the region's best farms, such as the Turners' Kinloch.

There were even shortages of wood—because there was no way to transport it. The armies had taken every farm wagon they could find for their supply trains. Besides losing their livestock, farmers saw their fences destroyed by troops who used the rails for firewood. Union forces occupying Warrenton even took crosses from the graves of Confederate soldiers in the town cemetery and used them for firewood. At Salem, paling fences surrounding yards and gardens were torn down and carried away for the same purpose.

It became nearly impossible to get medicines, and both soldiers and civilians died in outbreaks of scarlet fever, measles, smallpox, and pneumonia. Troops searched for wild onions and sassafras to ward off scurvy, and eventually Lee was forced to send troops into less devastated southeastern Virginia to forage for his army.

Around major battlefields, nearly every church, school, and home became a hospital or recovery shelter. Communities miles from the fighting were flooded with casualties as well. In Gordonsville, the Exchange Hotel was taken over by the Confederate government in the spring of 1862 and converted into a major receiving hospital. In one month, it admitted 6,000 patients, and in its busiest year it cared for 23,000. Those who died were buried in nearby fields. To the south, Albemarle County saw little fighting, but it was

St. Paul's Church in Haymarket was used by both Union and Confederate forces during the Civil War, serving as a hospital and as a stable. Common graves around the building hold casualties from both battles at Manassas as well as victims of a measles epidemic that struck in 1861, while the area was held by the Confederacy.

similarly inundated by the sick and wounded from the north. Charlottesville General Hospital, during the four years, admitted 21,540 patients, most of them suffering battle wounds. In many towns, nearly every able-bodied woman took up nursing duties, besides assuming jobs formerly reserved for white men—and for slaves.

From an upstairs window in this house, the Confederate guerilla leader John S. Mosby climbed into a walnut tree to avoid capture by a Union patrol. The house still stands, as does the walnut tree, but the limb that saved Mosby was cut off years ago.

✻ ✻ ✻

IN THE LAST TWO YEARS of the war, John Mosby's brazen harassment of Union troops and supply lines made him an idol of Confederates and their sympathizers and one of the men most wanted by federal authorities.

On a winter night in 1863, he and twenty-nine rangers rode into federally occupied Fairfax Courthouse, kidnapped Union general Edwin H. Stoughton from his bed, and escaped without a shot being fired. He wrecked the Manassas Gap Railroad so often and intimidated repair crews so thoroughly that the Union army finally gave up on keeping the line to the Shenandoah Valley in operation. During one six-month period he and his rangers killed, wounded, or captured a thousand Union officers and men and made off with hundreds of horses and mules while suffering fewer than a dozen casualties.

A fearless, instinctive warrior, Mosby was wounded three times, and several times rumored to be dead. Every time Union forces seemed to have him within their grasp, he got away. His command grew from nine riders to a cavalry battalion, and Mosby struck so often that he seemed to be in more than one place at a time.

Defenders of Washington became concerned that he might even try to kidnap President Lincoln or members of the cabinet, and began removing the plank flooring of Chain Bridge at night to prevent Mosby from slipping across the Potomac.

Trapped early one morning in the barnyard of a Loudoun County farm where he and about seventy of his men had spent the night, Mosby ran through a hail of bullets, opened a gate for troops to escape, and led a counter charge. When it was over, nine Vermont cavalrymen had been killed, more than a dozen wounded, and eighty taken prisoner. Mosby's men had also captured nearly a hundred Yankee horses. Only one of their own men had been killed and just a handful wounded.

On another occasion when Mosby's wife, Pauline, was visiting him at a friend's home near The Plains, a Union patrol arrived and raced up the stairs to the visitors' bedroom. Mrs. Mosby was found alone in bed, and a pair of the ranger's spurs lay on the floor, but there was no sign of Mosby himself. An instant earlier, he had jumped from a window into a walnut tree beside the house, and there he hid while all the farm's outbuildings were searched.

When Union forces executed seven Mosby troopers, hanging two of them with a warning of a similar fate for other rangers, the Gray Ghost responded in kind. Blaming George Custer for the executions, Mosby ordered the execution of an equal number of Custer's men outside a Union camp in the Shenandoah Valley.

In November 1864, Mosby's bedevilment of Union forces finally brought massive retribution against Loudoun and Fauquier County farms.

Mosby established himself as the nemesis of Federal forces in northern Virginia by kidnapping a Union general from this house in Union-occupied Fairfax. Such escapades made the Rebel cavalryman a vastly romanticized figure in Confederate folklore.

Under orders from Union Cavalry commander Philip Sheridan to punish the "hotbed of lawless bands," a federal division from the Shenandoah Valley swept the area from the Manassas Gap railroad north to the Potomac and as far east as the Bull Run Mountains, an area that had escaped massive damage. In four days of destruction, the so-called burning raids claimed hundreds of barns, thousands of tons of hay, thousands of bushels of grain, and numerous mills. About one thousand hogs were slaughtered, and when the Union troops went back across the Blue Ridge, they drove as many as six thousand head of cattle, four thousand sheep, and seven hundred horses. Ironically, the impact had fallen most heavily upon German and Quaker farmers loyal to the Union, and it would take decades for the area to recover.

On April 21, 1865, twelve days after Lee's surrender to Grant at Appomattox, Mosby assembled his rangers on a fog-shrouded field at Salem. He still was not willing to surrender, so he merely disbanded the battalion, freeing his men to accept individual federal paroles and return to their families.

At first suspected of complicity in President Lincoln's assassination,

ABOVE AND LEFT In the sanctuary of the Old Ebenezer Church in Loudoun County, John S. Mosby's rangers divided a $173,000 payroll taken when they wrecked a Union train in October 1863. Mosby declined to take his $2,000 share of the loot, but his men bought him a thorough-bred horse. The church, a Baptist meeting house constructed sometime between 1755 and 1769, stands in the community of Bloomfield, in the midst of an area known as "Mosby's Confederacy."

Mosby himself had a five-thousand-dollar price on his head, and for two months he remained a fugitive. Only after the personal intercession of General Grant did the government agree to consider him a free man. He later would infuriate Confederate diehards by becoming a Republican out of gratitude to the former Union army commander.

Mosby and his men returned to civilian life in a region not only wasted by warfare and military occupation, but spiritually and psychologically changed.

Slavery was dead. Many of the African Americans had gone north early in the war, and now others followed. Many moved into old and new freedmen's communities. More than five thousand black Virginians had joined the Union army. After the Emancipation Proclamation, former slaves who enlisted in the federal ranks guarded General Grant's supply train at the Battle of the Wilderness and suffered 1,300 casualties during the siege of Petersburg. With the fall of Richmond, black troops marched into the Confederate capital as the city's free African Americans cheered and danced in the streets.

Blacks and whites alike faced a long and painful reconstruction, but the country had been saved.

As historian David McCullough later observed, the change was most simply and eloquently reflected in the language itself. No longer did people write and say, "the United States are . . ." Universally, we still say, "the United States is . . ."

Recovery of the Piedmont took more than a generation. But in time, old manor houses were restored, fences were rebuilt, farms were reclaimed from the weeds, and saplings grew amid dead stumps.

Some land-poor Virginians had no recourse but to sell off their property. Those who stayed were more passionately attached to the soil and the Piedmont landscape than ever before.

When the scars had healed, the landscape was more lovely than it had been before war, and so it would remain until the late twentieth century, when it would be permanently changed.

St. Stephen's Church, near Catlett, was burned to the ground during the Civil War, but the congregation was held together by the leadership of the Ladies Sewing Society. A new sanctuary was consecrated in 1880.

Piedmont communities such as The Plains took years to recover from the Civil War, but in the twentieth century they rebounded with the help of a vibrant livestock industry and the region's emergence as prime horse breeding and foxhunting country. Today, the countryside is threatened by accelerating urban sprawl.

Summer lightning in Fauquier County.

Landscape in Peril

✳ ✳ ✳

IN NOVEMBER 1993, AFTER WEEKS OF SECRET DELIBERATIONS, THE Walt Disney Company rocked northern Virginia with an announcement that it planned a 3,000-acre, $650-million real estate development outside the Prince William County hamlet of Haymarket. Its centerpiece was to be a theme park called Disney's America. There the company planned to use a sweeping presentation of history as an attraction for millions of tourists. To most in the community of 483 residents, the prospect was Glorious. Haymarket would be on The Map. Prince William County would be in the clover. As many as 6 million tourists armed with heavy wallets would be coming from all over the world every year. There hadn't been such a big story in Haymarket since the Battle of Second Manassas just down the road in 1862.

But environmentalists, historians, and many longtime residents of farms and old towns across the Piedmont took Disney's announcement as a prescription for disaster. Their resistance set off a controversy that resonated in communities far from the Piedmont and caused northern Virginians to more seriously contemplate the future of their region.

Disney's plan was to tap directly into one of the country's most lucrative tourist markets—an annual tide of 20 million visitors drawn to the nation's capital just thirty-five miles away. These were people who appreciated history, families who spent vacations visiting the seat of government, exploring museums such as the famed Smithsonian Institution, and touring the nation's most treasured landmarks, including the Civil War battlefields of northern Virginia. Disney executives saw a history theme park as a natural addition to such a vacation itinerary.

At first blush, it seemed the company that had transformed cartoon characters into international personalities and made itself an American icon had scored another coup.

Dulles International Airport, undergoing a multi-million-dollar expansion, was only half an hour away. Interstate 66 ran along the southern boundary of the proposed Disney site. U.S. Route 15, the old Carolina Road, was on its eastern border, and there was already talk of making the historic corridor an interstate-style bypass around Washington. Land speculators and real

On 3,000 acres of this landscape, the Walt Disney Company proposed to build hundreds of houses, plus hotels, golf courses, and a theme park that would draw six million visitors a year.

The open country near Dulles International Airport,
bounded by Interstate 66 and only thirty-five miles from
Washington, D.C., seemed a perfect site. To Disney's
surprise, many Virginians disagreed.

estate agents rejoiced at the Disney news, as did local business owners, highway contractors, and entrepreneurs. Prince William County officials, hardpressed for new revenues to offset the highest county property taxes in Virginia, opened their arms. And an enthusiastic new governor, backed by a legislative majority, opened the state purse, agreeing to provide $163 million for construction of access roads and a new I-66 interchange.

Opponents of Disney's America take their protests to the shadow of the Capitol dome.

But less than a year after unveiling its proposal, Disney announced that it was striking its tent at Haymarket. Local business boosters were disconsolate, and avid political supporters were furious, feeling Disney had walked away just when it was about to clear its most significant obstacles.

Those who had looked askance at Disney's America—preservationists, land-use planners, environmentalists, historians, owners of the old estates and horse farms, and Virginians at large—saw hope in the project's demise. In their minds, the furor over the development had highlighted pervasive threats to the treasured landscape, raised consciousness about urban sprawl, and verified an urgent need for regional planning.

✴ ✴ ✴

THE LOCATION DISNEY HAD CHOSEN lay in the midst of an area that was extraordinarily rich in history. Within an easy drive of the site are sixteen Civil War battlefields, thirteen historic towns, and seventeen historic districts. The Manassas National Battlefield Park boundary is as little as three and a half miles away. All around spreads one of America's priceless rural landscapes, a region listed by the National Trust for Historic Preservation as one of the most endangered in the country.

Piedmont valleys that had sent men and boys to fight in the Revolution are still being farmed. Churches that sheltered the wounded of the Civil War still echo with the same hymns that were sung on Sunday mornings 150 years ago. In communities such as Stevensburg and Thoroughfare reside descendants of slaves, former indentured servants, and free blacks who numbered among the towns' settlers.

"It is one of the few places left in the eastern United States that still has a definable sense of place," says Ed McMahon, director of the Conservation Fund's American Greenways program. "In the Piedmont of northern Virginia, you still feel a connection with the land that you feel in very few other places. It is as close as you will ever get in this country to what the countryside in rural England is like."

The landscape evokes a simpler time: winding country lanes, stone houses, grist mills, revolutionary-period villages, and fields and meadows surrounded by stone fences. In the spring and fall, ridges, byways, stream banks, and mountain slopes explode with dazzling colors as farmlands turn green and then gold.

Along the eastern foothills of the Blue Ridge, gentle climate and hospitable soil sustain lush orchards and support vineyards that make the Piedmont a potential Napa Valley of the East. Half of Virginia's forty-six wineries are here in the uplands stretching northward from Monticello. Along with the orchards and fall foliage, they have become an important attraction for increasing numbers of tourists who explore the backroads and spend idyllic October weekends at secluded bed-and-breakfast inns.

The success of the wineries did not come quickly or easily. Like battlefields and historic houses, vineyards are a part of the Piedmont's heritage. Thomas Jefferson introduced European wines to his guests at Monticello and tried unsuccessfully to produce European varieties in his own vineyard. Claret produced near Charlottesville gained far-reaching acclaim before the Civil War, but the young vines died of inattention during the conflict, and the region fell into a century of vinicultural obscurity.

The scenic charms of the Piedmont are displayed along scores of country byways, and they are never more gorgeous than in mid-autumn.

ABOVE New prosperity for an old crop.

RIGHT Wine makers have found the soils of Piedmont and Blue Ridge slopes hospitable to their vines and the climate kind to the fruit. This family-run winery at Linden in Fauquier County has orchards as well as vines.

✣ ✣ ✣

IT WAS CONCERN FOR THE ENVIRONMENT, as much as attachment to history, that provoked resistance to Disney's plan. Just ten days after Disney first outlined its proposal, the Piedmont Environmental Council, which had been working more than twenty years to protect the rural Piedmont landscape, began a campaign urging the company to "take a second look." Simultaneously, it started raising a war chest for an expensive and protracted struggle whose outcome was anything but certain.

Soon, no fewer than seventy-five organizations had joined the fray. Opponents of Disney's real estate plans ranged from grassroots committees, such as Protect Prince William, to the National Trust for Historic Preservation and Protect Historic America, a committee led by a host of the country's leading historians. They included environmental groups, such as Clean Water Action and Audubon Naturalist Society, whose staff members joined the Piedmont Environmental Council in lobbying a Virginia legislature that was being fervently courted by emissaries from Disney.

The opposition ranks also included seasoned veterans of battles that had

already saved historic sites. Notable among them was Annie Snyder, a Gainesville activist who had organized the Save the Battlefield Coalition in the late eighties and had blocked a developer's plan to put a huge strip mall on the edge of the Manassas National Battlefield Park.

The involvement of historians across the country marked a turning point in the massively publicized debate. Led by nationally known figures such as David McCullough, James McPherson, Shelby Foote, C. Vann Woodward, John Hope Franklin, and William Styron, Protect Historic America helped transform a local land-use debate into a national issue. Their foremost concern was the destruction of historic places by an explosion of urban sprawl; in addition, many historians cringed at the thought of history being presented as an amusement.

Subtle, complex, and tragic events, they contended, were certain to be "plasticized" and romanticized beyond recognition. Disney, in their view, was about to destroy real history to create a simplistic, sugarcoated version of the nation's past.

Activists in all of the seventy-five anti-Disney groups regarded the theme park controversy as a crucial moment for a region already under relentless pressure and not yet organized to chart its own future. "There is a lot

ABOVE In a region famed as horse country, productive beef-cattle farms still thrive.

OPPOSITE In recent years, dairy farms, like this one in southern Fauquier County, have been rapidly replaced by development across much of northern Virginia.

151

more going on than the disappearance of farm fields," says Ed McMahon. "In the Piedmont, we are fighting for some sense of cultural continuity. If you lose the Piedmont, what is left? Where is the cultural continuity? Where is the psychological stability? Everybody, rich or poor, will share the loss."

Among the Piedmont Environmental Council's strategists, patrons, and allies were owners of Loudoun and Fauquier County estates where graceful old manor houses command panoramic views of the mountains and valleys. Some of the families had been in the Piedmont since before the Civil War. Some had arrived during the Reconstruction, others during the Great Depression, two periods when many old Virginians, finding themselves land-poor, were forced to sell off property.

Others with fortunes had been attracted to an area known as the greatest foxhunting country in America and home to some of the country's finest horseflesh. Family wealth, old and new, had helped preserve the landscape across the decades. Wealth meant large individual land holdings and low-intensity farming, tens of thousands of acres in hayfields and pasture for horse and beef-cattle farms.

Foxhunting became popular in the Piedmont in colonial times, and before the Civil War, the region had become known as the home of fine horses. Upperville's Piedmont Hunt, oldest of a dozen active organized foxhunts in northern Virginia, was established in 1840, and the annual Upperville Colt and Horse Show began in 1853.

Shortly after the turn of the century, railroad baron E. H. Harriman and several of his Wall Street associates moved their hounds from Orange County, New York, to The Plains to take advantage of Virginia's more favorable hunting weather. Over the years that followed, more of the first families of American business and finance would acquire estates in Loudoun and Fauquier Counties. The names included DuPont, Mellon, Warburg, and Whitney.

In more recent times, the foxhunting community has come to include residents who made their names in the military, the theater, and even politics. General Billy Mitchell, the father of the modern Air Force, lived in retirement in Middleburg, and George S. Patton was master of hounds at the now-defunct Cobbler Hunt long before he achieved World War II fame. Shortly after entering the White House, President John F. Kennedy leased Glen Ora, an estate two miles outside Middleburg, and only months before his death, he built Wexford, his own Piedmont retreat near Rattlesnake Mountain.

Opposition to Disney's America was hardly limited to the estate owners, hunters, historians, and environmental activists. Many residents of small towns feared a huge influx that would destroy the atmosphere they cherished. Workers who commuted from the Piedmont to Washington or its inner suburbs predicted gridlocked traffic. Taxpayers questioned official forecasts of an enhanced regional economy.

Their concerns were well-founded. A detailed study of land-use patterns and development in northern Virginia, commissioned by Protect Historic America in 1994, concluded that the theme park, and the hotels and massive housing developments Disney planned to build around it, would form the core of a huge new "edge city," equivalent in size to all the seventeen others around Washington combined.

Within twenty years, the study found, the Disney complex would produce a population surge of 230,000, swamping a transportation system that was already overburdened and without money available for a huge backlog of planned improvement projects. The additional sprawl, the study continued, would obliterate nationally significant cultural and historic resources, not to mention farmlands and other open spaces.

ABOVE Virginians and their hounds have chased foxes since colonial times. The Piedmont Hunt, organized in Upperville in 1840, is considered the oldest organized hunt in the country.

OPPOSITE At Manassas National Battlefield Park, visitors can now experience the countryside much as it was before the devastation caused by the war. Civil War battlefields have helped to make the Piedmont one of America's favorite tourist destinations, but sites without official protection are increasingly threatened.

*Melrose Castle was con-
structed in 1825, of stone
quarried around the
community of Casanova.
In 1863, following the
Battle of Gettysburg,
Union troops camped on
the castle's lawn as the war
moved back into Virginia.*

154

There were, moreover, profound questions concerning air and water quality and the adequacy of the water supply. Northern Virginia was already failing to comply with federal clean air standards, and estimates were that Disney's America would generate an additional 77,000 car trips on already crowded roads each day. As Prince William County officials and the Virginia state government worked to clear the way for Disney, resistance to the plan spread. Across the country, cartoonists ridiculed the project. Columnists and editorial writers attacked the company for lacking sensitivity and questioned whether seasonal, low-paying jobs provided by the theme park would help the local economy.

Rush-hour traffic out of Washington and its suburbs crawls westward on Interstate 66 in Prince William County. The scene is increasingly familiar in every corner of the Piedmont as cities such as Charlottesville and Richmond generate their own urban sprawl.

"It is astonishing that Disney, out of sheer stubbornness, is risking its reputation as a good corporate citizen," wrote syndicated columnist George Will, "and is doing so to put here a project that could be put in many more suitable places."

Avid supporters of the project, including public officials and private citizens, sought to dismiss the opposition as a collection of activists led by the Piedmont Environmental Council, blindly fighting growth and progress. Historians, such as Shelby Foote, who warned that Disney's America would plasticize history, were characterized as elitists. Owners of estates and horse farms were accused of fighting for narrow self interests.

Nine months after its dramatic announcement of Disney's America, the company dropped its Haymarket plans without warning, saying it would look elsewhere for a home for Disney's America. "We remain convinced that a park that celebrates America and an exploration of our heritage is a great idea, and we will continue to work to make it a reality," said the official announcement. "However, we recognize that there are those who have been concerned about the possible impact of our park on historic sites in this unique area, and we have always tried to be sensitive to the issue."

Analysts who had followed the episode speculated about a variety of possible Disney motives for changing course. Most concluded that the company had underestimated potential opposition at the beginning. They also agreed that the controversy had shown how seriously the Piedmont is threatened by a host of forces. The struggle to preserve the region's rural character had been energized, at least temporarily.

"We don't have to save every blade of grass of the Piedmont, but we must preserve its essential character," says Richard Moe, president of the National

Surrounded by its lush gardens, the Oak Hill estate created by James Monroe remains an island of seclusion. But many remote farms and estates are yielding to breakup and random development as edge cities and "mini-estates" march across the landscape of the rural Piedmont

Dawn in the Piedmont. Beyond the sprawl of exurbia, a rural landscape and a rural culture survive under duress.

In a valley outside Leesburg, lights twinkle from a new town-house community recently risen on a former Loudon County farm.

Trust for Historic Preservation, "and that means its wonderful small towns, its historic sites, and the landscape itself."

✱ ✱ ✱

NATIVES HARDLY NEED REMINDING of the threat to their communities, heritage, and land. Nor do relative newcomers who have watched two decades of explosive growth. The region lies at the doorstep of the fourth largest urban complex in America—Baltimore, Washington, and their spreading suburbs and edge cities. Near the two cities are some of the more affluent jurisdictions in the United States.

One of them, Fairfax County, in the eastern Piedmont, epitomizes what has happened. In scarcely more than a generation, it has changed nearly beyond recognition. Dairy farms, truck farms, and small towns were relentlessly overrun or surrounded by a seamless web of megamalls, housing developments, and superhighways. Between 1950 and 1990, the county's population soared from fewer than 100,000 to nearly 900,000—surpassing that of seven different states, including Delaware, Vermont, and Wyoming. By the early 1990s, its budget had surpassed $1 billion. The summit of a mammoth sanitary landfill had become the highest point of land in the county. The last remaining dairy farm was being run by and for a prison.

Robert T. Dennis, who served as president of the Piedmont Environmental Council for fourteen years, wistfully recalls growing up in a small Fairfax County village in the fifties. It was a place that still had some unpaved streets. Dennis awoke in the morning to hear roosters crowing and cows lowing in the fields nearby. "Today, it exists in name only," he says. "It's called Falls Church."

Loudoun County residents, watching the rapid approach of exurban Washington in the 1970s, took up the refrain "Don't Fairfax Loudoun." But today its eastern section has become indistinguishable from the sprawl of Fairfax, even though the county was one of the first in the nation to adopt a comprehensive development plan. Eastern Prince William met a similar fate. Several miles south of Washington, it boasts one of the busiest tourist destinations in Virginia—

a gigantic factory outlet mall that attracts busloads from all over the mid-Atlantic.

Fauquier County, having gone for nearly a century without appreciable population growth, saw modest growth in the 1960s, followed by a surge of 36 percent in the seventies and another 36 percent in the eighties.

Apace with the urbanization, the political landscape changed as well. With county political power increasingly concentrated in heavily populated districts, county governments became more focused on their urban problems. Consequently, some residents of the more rural areas have even fantasized about bringing together the less populated, agricultural sections of Fauquier, western Prince William, western Loudoun, and possibly Clarke Counties to form a new county.

Pressures imposed by booming growth and development do not end with the creep of shopping malls and subdivisions from Washington's outer suburbs into eastern Loudoun and Prince William Counties.

More vexing to land-use planners and officials in rural areas is the proliferation of five- and ten-acre lots that rapidly gobble up farms and open landscapes. Oversized houses on five-acre lots have erupted like measles across Fauquier, western Loudoun, western Prince William, and Spotsylvania Counties, their architecture often jarringly inappropriate to a rural setting. Richmond and Charlottesville have become dynamos for the same kind of sprawl in Albemarle, Greene, Louisa, and Madison Counties, and beyond the Piedmont.

ABOVE A few minutes from congested traffic, shopping centers, and suburban noise, the charm of the rural Piedmont endures.

PAGES 162-163 In Rappahannock County, where the rural landscape has been well preserved, a country road little changed over the last century leads toward the Blue Ridge.

Transactions leading to such development were set in motion in the 1960s with the arrival of land speculators attracted by Dulles Airport and plans for Interstate 66. The speculators were followed by waves of developers in the seventies and eighties. Some rural areas, such as Rappahannock County, saw land prices zoom from $100 per acre to $1,000 per acre within two or three years.

Ninety-three-year-old Thomas O. Madden Jr. of Culpeper County still lives on Elkwood farm, where his great-grandfather, a free black man, prospered against all odds during slavery. Madden has told the saga of his remarkable family, descended from an African father and a European mother, in the book We Were Always Free.

Residential development widely scattered across open spaces requires huge public subsidies in the form of sewer lines, new roads, and fleets of school buses. The most common, but unsuccessful, remedy for this suburban sprawl, says James Howard Kunstler, author of *The Geography of Nowhere,* "is large lot zoning."

"People devised it thinking it was going to give them a countrylike setting, but what it really gives them has none of the benefits of town life and none of the characteristics of country life. All you get is a yard that's too big to mow and too small to plow, and no sense of a neighborhood. We know this doesn't work. We know that it's not making people happy. We know that the cost of servicing these subdivisions is bankrupting our towns."

The fight to head off random sprawl in the rural Piedmont involves both public and private strategies. Fauquier County requires that 85 percent of a given rural parcel be kept open. This means that a landowner with 1,000 acres can subdivide 150 of them. Albemarle County has a similar sliding scale arrangement. Rappahannock County, under less severe development pressure, mandates a minimum lot size of twenty-five acres. Rural counties elsewhere have used yet another tack, setting a maximum lot size of about two acres.

Efforts to protect the landscape go back to the late 1960s when private landowners began putting property into open space easements, most held by the Virginia Outdoors Foundation, and into agricultural and forestal districts to prevent development.

Leading the stepped-up private conservation movement, the Piedmont Environmental Council in 1984 adopted a goal of protecting a million acres in its nine-county area. A decade later, 400,000 acres are protected by scenic or conservation easement, public ownership, or location with agricultural or forestal districts.

Huge expanses in northern Fauquier and western Loudoun Counties and in the Southwest Mountains of Albemarle County lie in the protected areas. They include some of the region's most beautiful landscape and most

cherished historical sites. Northern Fauquier and western Loudoun are pep-
pered with houses, churches, and other sites linked to Mosby's Confederacy.
The Southwest Mountains run between Jefferson's Monticello and James
Madison's Montpelier, and Jefferson descendants live in the area even now.
Immediately to the east of the mountains, the countryside looks a great deal
as it did in the days when Jefferson and Madison traveled it. Within the
35,000 acres of the Southwest Mountains Historic District, some 12,000
acres have been put into open space easements.

While the Piedmont Environmental Council is the area's most influential regional environmental organization, it does not labor alone. Other
groups formed in the face of specific threats have become stalwarts in pro-
moting sensible land use and resource conservation. Citizens for Fauquier,
founded in the early seventies, succeeded in stopping an Arkansas developer
from building a housing project that would have covered 4,200 acres and virtually doubled the county's population in one fell swoop. The Goose Creek
Association saved a historic stream threatened by pollution from a nursing
home. Friends of Bull Run prevented development from spoiling one of the
region's prettiest mountain ridges.

The falls of the Rappahannock stopped the first English sailing ships carrying explorers into Virginia, and the white water above Fredericksburg still challenges canoeists. In river bends and coves upstream, bass fishermen confront a different kind of test and find their own rewards.

The Hidden Inn, a landmark in the town of Orange, now offers bed and breakfast to paying guests. Continuously occupied since its construction as a farmhouse in 1880, it was restored a decade ago. All across the Piedmont, other historic houses have become stopping places for visitors — modern, often luxurious versions of the eighteenth- and nineteenth-century ordinaries.

Historians and environmentalists have waged a long war to save this Culpeper County farmland, the site of the Battle of Brandy Station, the largest cavalry engagement of the entire war. Some of the troopers who died were buried where they fell.

And without attracting the kind of attention that surrounded the debate over Disney's America, other struggles to preserve the Piedmont landscape and heritage continue.

Since 1990, the Brandy Station Foundation and its allies in the historical community have fought to save the battlefield where the largest cavalry engagement of the Civil War was waged. A California developer's plan for a huge office complex on the land ended in bankruptcy in 1993.

But soon thereafter, other interests proposed to put an automobile racetrack on fields where Confederate and Union cavalry units suffered hundreds of casualties and dozens are believed to be buried.

Like the debate over Disney's America, the fate of the Brandy Station battlefield provoked bitter divisions within the local community. Hoping to preserve the site as a park, the Brandy Station Foundation, the Association for the Protection of Civil War Sites, and other supporters offered $5 million for 2,300 acres of the property. The proposal was rejected, as was the Association's offer of $2.1 million for 425 acres where the racetrack was planned.

ABOVE AND OPPOSITE Mrs. Sally Witten has lived at Auburn, her farm in Culpeper County, since 1915. Her daughter, granddaughter, and great-granddaughter have all been married there, wearing her wedding dress. The Battle of Brandy Station was fought nearby, and during the course of the Civil War, both Robert E. Lee and Ulysses S. Grant reviewed troops encamped on the estate.

In the fall of 1995, the racetrack venture also fell into bankruptcy. With that, the Brandy Station Foundation and the Association for the Protection of Civil War Sites entered into new negotiations with the property owner, offering $6 million for 1,500 acres of the battleground. It appeared that the area would at last be protected.

More famous Piedmont battlefields are threatened by traffic and development even though they are national parks. At Chancellorsville and the Wilderness, housing developments come within feet of Civil War earthworks. At Manassas, U.S. Routes 29 and 234, which intersect in the battlefield, have evolved from country lanes into commuter roads used by nearly 50,000 motorists every day.

What threatens the future of the Piedmont as much as the sprawl of subdivisions and malls is relentless pressure for more high-speed commuter roads and new transportation corridors.

Foremost on the agenda of strategic planners is a superhighway allowing interstate traffic to elude the congestion of the notorious Capital Beltway encircling Washington. Once envisioned as an "outer beltway," the new corridor has come to be referred to as a bypass. A western route would pass

through the Piedmont, an eastern route would pass through Maryland. In the former, Virginia preservationists see the specter of destruction for historic and scenic treasures. Critics contend that construction of both bypasses, at a cost of perhaps $3 billion, would not significantly reduce congestion on the present beltway.

Possible western bypass scenarios include turning venerable corridors, such as U.S. Route 17, between Fredericksburg and Warrenton, and U.S. Route 15 in northern Fauquier and Loudoun Counties, into limited-access freeways with high-speed interchanges. Constructed piecemeal, these could become components of the long-debated bypass. Route 15, once an Indian path and later a major avenue for the marching armies of the Civil War, passes near Oak Hill, the home of James Monroe, near the historic Oatlands plantation outside Leesburg, and through lovely Loudoun County farms before crossing the Potomac into Maryland. It is among the 1,200 miles of Virginia roads designated as scenic byways by the Virginia Department of Transportation.

Similarly daunting is the possibility that U.S. Route 29, running from Washington through Warrenton, Culpeper, and Charlottesville, will be turned into an interstate-style corridor. A significant step in that direction came

PAGES 172-173 Travelers crossing Ashby's Gap from the Shenandoah Valley into the Piedmont first see Paris Valley nestled against the foothills of the Blue Ridge. The area gets its name from the hamlet of Paris near the junction of U. S. Highways 50 and 17.

One of the best-known land-marks of the Virginia hunt country, Middleburg's Red Fox Inn has hosted civil war strategy meetings, visiting celebrities, and newspaper reporters covering President John F. Kennedy.

Oatlands Plantation, near Leesburg, is a showplace from the nineteenth century now owned by the National Trust for Historic Preservation.

when it was given a high-priority designation in the National Highway System contemplated by Congress.

Constructing a Washington bypass and turning U.S. 29 into a high-speed corridor between Washington and Greensboro, North Carolina, are only two of many proposals being considered by state and federal planners and the trucking and road-building industries. Environmentalists have other reasons to be concerned. By going through the Piedmont, trucks traveling to Norfolk from the industrial centers of the West Virginia and Pennsylvania region could avoid a slow and expensive journey through the immediate Washington area or a long trip down the Shenandoah Valley.

Less dramatic projects pose their own threats. Furious residents of Rappahannock County crowded into a public hearing to protest the very suggestion of widening to six lanes a portion of Route 211, the highway crossing the county between Warrenton and the Shenandoah Valley. At the same time, residents of Loudoun County mounted a determined campaign against plans to widen a stretch of Route 50 on the eastern side of the county. The route was the main street of Mosby's Confederacy, passing through Aldie, Middleburg, and Upperville on its way to Ashby's Gap and the Shenandoah Valley.

Although growing numbers of commuters, the promise of jobs, and the support of developers make road-building projects powerfully seductive to political officials, they are not irresistible.

Residents along Snickersville Pike battled the Virginia Department of Transportation to a standstill after it moved to widen and straighten the old road connecting the towns of Aldie and Bluemont. George Washington traveled the route on his way to the Shenandoah Valley, and during the road-building boom of the early nineteenth century, it became a privately owned turnpike.

The backroads of the Piedmont provide weekend escape for growing numbers of urban dwellers, particularly during the spring and fall.

With the scenic lane in danger of being ruined, a handful of residents formed the Snickersville Turnpike Association to oppose its obliteration in the name of progress. Their efforts caused Scenic America, a non-profit conservation group, to list the pike—along with Route 15—among the nation's ten most endangered byways.

But still highway engineers have not given up on modernizing the road, and the Snickersville Turnpike Association has vowed to fight on indefinitely.

❋ ❋ ❋

DISNEY'S DECISION TO ABANDON ITS PROJECT at Haymarket left northern Virginia with a hangover. State legislators and local officials who had backed the project felt betrayed, and opponents' joy was tempered by the knowledge that they had won only a momentary triumph in a war with no foreseeable end.

It was clear that without a regional strategy and regional tactics, the rural landscape of the northern Piedmont eventually would be lost. Historic preservation and land-use issues had become too complex to be resolved by factions that casually dismissed each other as pro-growth or anti-growth.

"The Piedmont is going to grow," says Ed McMahon. "The question is how. Where do you put the growth? How do you arrange it so that it respects the character of the place? Voluntary conservation is not enough. Zoning is not enough. The only thing that can save the Piedmont is a shared vision."

The ruins of Barboursville have stood unreclaimed since Christmas Day, 1884, when the mansion built by former Virginia governor James Barbour was swept by fire. The house was designed for Barbour by his friend Thomas Jefferson after Jefferson left the White House.

*Beneath a hot summer sun, archaeologists at Montpelier
search for remains of a blacksmith shop constructed by
James Madison, Sr., father of the nation's fourth president.
The domed structure in the background is the estate's "ice
house palace." Beneath it is the ice house constructed by
President Madison after he inherited Montpelier.*

In the winter and spring after the Disney crisis ended, the search for a shared vision began. Veterans of the battle against the theme park convened a series of meetings to look ahead.

Among the participants was Hope Porter, one of those who organized Citizens for Fauquier when the county faced its first urban sprawl crisis nearly

The Piedmont's reputation as "horse country" was made by thoroughbreds, but bulky, less glamorous draft horses helped to make the Piedmont frontier prime farmland. Today, they can be seen demonstrating their power in pulling contests such as this one at Oatlands in Loudoun County.

a quarter century ago. "I think we are going to look back upon Disney as having been the best thing that ever happened," she said. "It was a wakeup call, and it was just extraordinary how people reacted all over the United States. It showed that there is a deep, deep love for this country."

Ironically, it was Disney, thwarted in its plans for the history park, that led a whole generation of newcomers to become acquainted with the Piedmont's storied past. The debate renewed Virginians' consciousness of their heritage; it sharpened the Piedmont's identity and gave it new meaning as a special place.

The Piedmont is a region whose full story is still being written. Historians continue to add Civil War sites to the National Register of Historic Places. Archaeologists still sift through the ruins of Native American villages and English settlements, seeking to learn more about the area's early inhabitants.

Along the Rapidan River, near the boundary between Orange and Greene Counties, scholars have excavated a Monacan burial mound and human bones dating back to A.D. 900. In Orange County, archaeologists are carefully exposing the remains of the old Germanna fortress and the nearby foundation of Alexander Spotswood's "Enchanted Castle," the mansion where the colorful lieutenant governor lived in retirement. In Charlottesville, anthropologists are unearthing buildings and household objects from a forgotten community of free African Americans that took root more than forty years before the Civil War.

And in the countryside, a farmer or a hunter still occasionally finds an arrowhead, a brass button, or a minié ball, or discovers a lonely grave.

ABOVE On a peaceful hillside in Greene County rest the families who once tended the fields beyond.

PAGES 182-83 Settled in 1733, the Quaker village of Waterford is officially designated a National Historic Landmark. It has no traffic lights and only a single grocery store.

PAGES 184-85 The Piedmont of northern Viginia is on the fringe of a megalopolis reaching from Boston to Richmond and Petersburg, but its rural areas still present panoramas such as this fog-shrouded landscape in Loudoun County.

THIS BOOK IS DEDICATED TO THE PEOPLE OF THE NORTHERN VIRGINIA PIEDMONT. To them is entrusted one of America's special places. To them has fallen a priceless legacy—a landscape of extraordinary beauty, visited by heroism and tragedy, a region tested and renewed. Before today's inhabitants of the Piedmont lies a daunting challenge: to pass along the historic and natural treasures of a region aptly called the "Cradle of Democracy."

These Virginians, their predecessors, and far-flung Americans with roots in the Old Dominion have helped to protect Civil War battlefields, save eighteenth- and nineteenth-century architectural gems, and preserve an enduringly lovely countryside. But with each passing year, burgeoning population and ill-planned and unplanned development pose mounting new threats to historic sites and rural communities.

In these pages, the author and two talented photographers have tried to evoke endearing qualities that distinguish the northern Virginia Piedmont. For faithful support in this endeavor, we are indebted to friends too numerous to name.

We especially wish to thank the members and leadership of the following organizations: the Piedmont Environmental Council, the Accokeek Foundation, the American Farmland Trust, the Audubon Naturalist Society, the Bluemont Citizens Association, the Brandy Station Foundation, the Cedar Run Alliance, the Chesapeake Bay Foundation, Citizens for Fauquier County, Clean Water Action, the Conservation Fund, Friends of Bull Run, Friends of Culpeper, the Goose Creek Association, the Mosby Heritage Area, the National Growth Management Leadership Project, the National Trust for Historic Preservation, Prince Charitable Trust, Protect Prince William, the Rappahannock League

for Environmental Protection, the Save the Battlefield Coalition, the Florence and John Schumann Foundation, the Sierra Club (Virginia chapter), the Snickersville Turnpike Association, and the Walden Woods Project.

One other group, Protect Historic America, deserves special mention. Founded in 1994 when the northern Piedmont was threatened by a proposed theme-park real-estate development, this committee, led by more than 200 of the country's most revered historians and history writers, launched a spirited national campaign on behalf of the region's historic sites. Opinion leaders, environmental activists, history buffs, and ordinary Americans rallied behind Shelby Foote, John Hope Franklin, David McCullough, James M. McPherson, W. Brown Morton, William Styron, Tom Wicker, C. Vann Woodward, and other members of Protect Historic America's advisory board.

Piedmont residents who inspired PHA were also the chief forces behind the creation of this volume. Foremost among them were Nick and Mary Lynn Kotz of Broad Run, Virginia, and Julian and Sue Scheer of Catlett, Virginia, and Richard Moe, president of the National Trust for Historic Preservation. Notable among their earliest unstinting allies was Peter Hannaford. All are due the thanks of Virginia and the country for what they have done to preserve the region's historic places and save its rural landscape. And finally, for their patience, perseverance, and innumerable contributions, we especially wish to thank Leonard Phillips, Deborah Sussman, and Nancy Kober.

Rudy Abramson   *Kenneth Garrett*   *Jack Kotz*
Reston, Virginia   Broad Run, Virginia   Santa Fe, New Mexico

Organizations

The following organizations belong to a growing list of groups that support protection of natural and historic resources of Virginia's northern Piedmont and preservation of its rural landscape.

Accokeek Foundation
3400 Bryan Point Road
Accokeek, MD 20607

Aldie Citizens Association
P. O. Box 117
Aldie, VA 20105

Alliance for Historic Landscape Preservation
Suite 1105
82 Wall Street
New York, NY 10005

American Farmland Trust
1920 N Street, N.W.
Washington, DC 20036

America the Beautiful Fund
219 Shoreham Building
806 15th Street, N.W.
Washington, DC 20005

Arlington Heritage Alliance
P. O. Box 1418
Arlington, VA 22210

Audubon Naturalist Society
8940 Jones Mill Road
Chevy Chase, MD 20815

Bluemont Citizens Association
Bluemont, VA 20135

Brandy Station Foundation
Post Office Box 165
Brandy Station, VA 22714

Cedar Run Alliance
P. O. Box 17
Sommerville, VA 22739

Chesapeake Bay Foundation
Suite 710
1001 East Main Street
Richmond, VA 23219

Clarke County Citizens Council
RT. 3, Box 5815
Berryville, VA 22611

Clean Water Action
Suite 300
1320 18th Street, N.W.
Washington, DC 20036

Citizens for Albemarle
P. O. Box 3751
Charlottesville, VA 22903-3751

Citizens for Fauquier County
P. O. Box 3486
Warrenton, VA 20186

Commonwealth Coalition
1542 Dry Run Road
Fort Valley, VA 22652

Conservation Fund
1800 North Kent Street
Arlington, VA 22209

Countryside Institute
P. O. Box 21380
Washington, DC 20009

Environmental Defense Fund
1875 Connecticut Avenue, N.W.
Washington, DC 20009

Friends of Bull Run
P.O. Box 402
The Plains, VA 20198

Friends of Culpeper
8208 Maple Lawn Lane
Rapidan, VA 22733

Friends of the Rappahannock
P. O. Box 7254
Fredericksburg, VA 22404

Friends of Warrenton
P. O. Box 3125
Warrenton, VA 20186

Garden Club of Virginia
12 East Franklin Street
Richmond, VA 23219

Goose Creek Association
P. O. Box 1178
Middleburg, VA 22117

Historic Fredericksburg
Foundation, Inc.
P. O. Box 8327
Fredericksburg, VA 22404

Izaak Walton League of America
707 Conservation Lane
Gaithersburg, MD 20878

John Singleton Mosby Heritage Area
P. O. Box 1178
Middleburg, VA 20117

League of Women Voters of the National Capital Area
1103 Dartmouth Road
Alexandria, VA 22314-4708

National Alliance of Preservation Commissions
Hall of States, Suite 342
444 North Capitol Street
Washington, DC 20001

National Alliance of Statewide
Preservation Organizations
c/o Preservation North Carolina
P.O. Box 27644
Raleigh, NC 27611

National Audubon Society
700 Broadway
New York, NY 10003

National Parks and Conservation Association
1776 Massachusetts Avenue, N.W.
Washington, DC 20036

National Trust for Historic Preservation
1785 Massachusetts Avenue, N.W.
Washington, DC 20036

National Wildlife Federation
1400 16th Street, N. W.
Washington, DC 20036

Natural Resources Defense Council
1350 New York Avenue, N.W.
Washington, DC 20005

Nature Conservancy (Virginia chapter)
1233 A Cedars Court
Charlottesville, VA 22903-4800

Piedmont Environmental Council
P. O. Box 460, 45 Horner Street
Warrenton, VA 20186

Preservation Action
1350 Connecticut Avenue, N.W.
Washington, DC 20036

Preservation Alliance of Virginia
P. O. Box 1407
Staunton, VA 24402-1407

Prince Charitable Trust
816 Connecticut Avenue, N.W.
Washington, DC 20006

Protect Prince William
P. O. Box 640
Haymarket, VA 22069

Ragged Mountain Resource Center
P. O. Box 141
Washington, VA 22747

Rappahannock League for Environmental Protection
Rt. 1, Box 425
Washington, VA 22747

Route 50 Corridor Coalition
Post Office Box 1555
Middleburg, VA 20117

Scenic America
21 DuPont Circle, N.W.
Washington, DC 20036

Florence and John Schumann Foundation
33 Park Street
Montclair, NJ 07042

Sierra Club (Virginia chapter)
P. O. Box 14648
Richmond, VA 23221-0648

Sierra Club
85 Second Street, 2nd Floor
San Francisco, CA 94105

Snickersville Turnpike Association
Post Office Box 808
Middleburg, VA 20117

Southern Environmental Law Center
201 West Main Street, Suite 14
Charlottesville, VA 22902

Surface Transportation Policy Project
1400 16th Street, N.W., Suite 300
Washington, DC 20036

Trout Unlimited Virginia Council
302 Danray Drive
Richmond, VA 23227

Trust for Public Land
Suite 401
666 Pennsylvania Avenue, S.E.
Washington, DC 20003

Valley Conservation Council
P. O. Box 2335
Staunton, VA 24402

Virginia Conservation Network
1001 East Broad Street, Suite 410
Richmond, VA 23219-1928

Virginia Native Plant Society
P. O. Box 844
Annandale, VA 22003

Walden Woods Project
18 Tremont Street, Suite 522
Boston, MA 02108

Waterford Foundation
P. O. Box 142
Waterford, VA 20197

Wilderness Society
900 17th Street, N.W.
Washington, DC 20006

Suggested Reading

Ammon, Harry. *JAMES MONROE: The Quest for National Identity.* Charlottesville: University Press of Virginia, 1990.

Beveridge, Albert J. *THE LIFE OF JOHN MARSHALL.* 4 vols. Boston and New York: Houghton Mifflin Co., 1916.

Brant, Irving. *THE FOURTH PRESIDENT: A Life of James Madison.* New York: The Bobbs-Merrill Co., Inc., 1970.

Collier, Christopher and James Lincoln Collier. *DECISION IN PHILADELPHIA: The Constitutional Convention of 1787.* New York: Ballantine Books, 1987.

Flexner, James Thomas. *WASHINGTON: The Indispensable Man.* Boston: Little, Brown and Co., 1969.

Freeman, Douglas Southall. *LEE'S LIEUTENANTS: A Study in Command.* 3 vols. New York: Charles Scribner's Sons, 1946.

Furgurson, Ernest B. *CHANCELLORSVILLE 1863: The Souls of the Brave.* New York: Alfred A. Knopf, 1992.

Goolrick, John T. *HISTORIC FREDERICKSBURG: The Story of an Old Town.* Richmond, Virginia: Whittet and Shepperson, 1922.

Gott, John K. *HIGH IN OLD VIRGINIA'S PIEDMONT: A History of Marshall (formerly Salem), Fauquier County, Virginia.* Marshall, Virginia: Marshall National Bank and Trust Co., 1987.

Harrison, Fairfax. *LANDMARKS OF OLD PRINCE WILLIAM,* Vol. I and II. Prince William County Historical Commission (reprint edition 1987).

Havinghurst, Walter. *ALEXANDER SPOTSWOOD: Portrait of a Governor.* New York: Holt, Rinehart and Winston, 1967.

Hennessy, John J. *RETURN TO BULL RUN: The Campaign and Battle of Second Manassas.* New York: Simon and Schuster, 1993.

Jefferson, Thomas. *NOTES ON THE STATE OF VIRGINIA.* New York: Torchbook, 1964.

Jones, Virgil Carrington. *RANGER MOSBY.* Chapel Hill: The University of North Carolina Press, 1944.

Madden, T.O., Jr., with Ann L. Miller. *WE WERE ALWAYS FREE: The Maddens of Culpeper County, Virginia: A 200-Year Family History.* New York: W. W. Norton Co., 1992.

Malone, Dumas. *THOMAS JEFFERSON AND HIS TIME.* 6 vols. Boston: Little Brown and Co., 1948.

McLaughlin, Jack. *JEFFERSON AND MONTICELLO: The Biography of a Builder.* New York: Henry Holt and Co., 1988.

Moffett, Lee. *THE DIARY OF COURTHOUSE SQUARE: Warrenton, Virginia, USA, From Early Times Through 1986.* Stephens City, Virginia: Commercial Press, 1988.

Rhea, Gordon C. *THE BATTLE OF THE WILDERNESS, May 5-6, 1864.* Baton Rouge: Louisiana State University Press, 1994.

Russell, T. Triplett and John K. Gott. *FAUQUIER COUNTY IN THE REVOLUTION.* Warrenton, Virginia: Warrenton Printing and Publishing Co., 1977.

Scheel, Eugene M. *CULPEPER: A Virginia County's History Through 1920.* Orange, Virginia: Green Publishers, Inc., 1982.

____. *THE HISTORY OF MIDDLEBURG AND VICINITY.* Middleburg, Virginia: Middleburg Bicentennial Committee, 1987.

Selby, John. *THE REVOLUTION IN VIRGINIA.* Williamsburg: Colonial Williamsburg Foundation, 1988.

Wert, Jeffry D. *MOSBY'S RANGERS.* New York: Simon and Schuster, 1991.

Index

Going to the Firemen's Parade in Flint Hill, Virginia.

Photography Credits

Kenneth Garrett: cover, pages 10-11, 22-23, 24, 27, 29, 30, 31, 32, 33, 35, 36-37, 38, 38-39, 42, 44, 46, 52-53, 66-67, 68, 69, 71, 72, 73, 76, 78, 84, 85, 87, 88-89, 91, 92, 93, 94-95, 99, 100-101, 102, 104-105, 107, 109, 115, 116, 117, 118-119, 120-121, 122, 124, 125,126, 127, 135, 140-141, 144, 145, 146, 147, 148, 148-149, 150, 151, 152, 153, 156, 158, 160, 161, 162-163, 166, 167, 168-169, 178-179, 180, 182-183, 184-185, 186, 187, 192.

Jack Kotz: endsheets, pages 2-3, 4-5, 6-7, 8-9, 12-13, 14, 16, 18, 26, 28, 34, 40-41, 45, 49, 50, 51, 55, 56, 57, 58, 58-59, 60, 61, 62, 63, 64, 70-71, 75, 80, 82, 86, 97, 108, 111, 112-113, 118, 128-129, 129, 130, 132-133, 134, 136-137, 137, 139, 142, 154, 157, 158-159, 164, 165, 170, 171, 172-173, 174-175, 176, 179, 181.